the ORGANIC ADVANTAGE

Master SEO and natural traffic generation
for your ecommerce business to
achieve reliable, sustainable growth

MARTIN HAYMAN

RETHINK PRESS

First published in Great Britain in 2019 by Rethink Press
(www.rethinkpress.com)

Cover image © Shutterstock | Vector Goddess

Contents

Introduction: My Story

When I was at college, I had ambitions to become a pilot. But things didn't quite go to plan for a number of reasons and that goal quickly faded into the distance. My experiences flying Chipmunks and Bulldogs and learning aerobatics during my Air Training Corps days will remain as amazing memories but in the end, things went in a quite different direction.

After a stint in telecoms, I found myself in the thrilling world of IT and once I'd gained some experience, I started my own IT support business in 2007 – just before the recession kicked in. Fantastic timing! There I was, trying to squeeze in sales, marketing and my actual job of supporting clients, while businesses were cutting their IT budgets. It didn't help that I hated any form of cold selling. Despite this, I managed to keep things going for two years and it was during this time that I started to get my head into the world of Search Engine Optimisation (SEO).

At the two-year mark, though, it was time to call it a day. Things weren't going anywhere and I also took the time to drop an honesty bomb: I hated what I was doing. I had no love for the work and I was never going to succeed at something I had no passion for.

A job came up at a media business that owned about eighty web properties. It was a junior SEO role and the money was low – but boy, am I glad I took the job, because that was the turning point. They were great at developing people and I learned a huge amount during my time there. And I loved what I was doing. When I moved to an agency in Brighton, I was able to apply what I'd learned there and I climbed into a senior role fairly quickly. The time I spent there was another great experience, working with some massive brands; after some time in this role I was invited back to the media business where it all started, to run their small digital marketing agency. It wasn't long before the group's Head of SEO left for Japan and the company asked me to fill the role. I then moved to a business on the south coast of England who had a small agency and a few ecommerce websites. Although this was a smaller business, their approach to online marketing was quite different and it was a good learning curve.

Leaving there to go freelance was a scary move, but an exciting one. I had been in the industry around a decade by that point and had made some good contacts; I already had a small pool of clients. I wanted to focus on ecommerce as that was where a lot of my experience sat. I also believed that my strong technical SEO experience could benefit larger national and international websites.

I decided early on that I wanted to grow my team using freelancers and partnerships. It's a model that works and enables me to build more flexible, skilled and specific teams for clients. As the team grew, it no longer made sense to call myself a freelancer. Wild Sprout was born. And today Wild Sprout helps ecommerce businesses and other large websites turn flatlines and declines into upward curves.

Why I wrote this book

When I talk to business owners, they often have similar questions; questions that show how hard it is to keep up with this ever-evolving industry. Some people still think of SEO as a magical quick fix. Some people still think you need to blog everyday – about anything, no matter how irrelevant – just to keep your content 'fresh'. Some people have had bad experiences with marketing services, often due to a lack of knowledge and a feeling that they were just being bombarded with excuses and buzzwords. I have also come across digital marketers and even small agencies whose knowledge is severely lacking.

I was asked to help train the team at one of these agencies to enable them to get better results for their clients. I wanted to write a book that would help people like this – a book that would bring people up to speed on what works today, and the strategies and tactics they can use most effectively. I also wanted the book to help those less knowledgeable to gain a better understanding of online marketing, putting them in a stronger position when they're talking to their internal teams or outsourced resources.

Who this book is for

Because I've worked with so many ecommerce business owners, ecommerce directors, marketing managers and those responsible for the online marketing of ecommerce websites, I've written this book with those groups particularly in mind, but its scope is broader than that. The book will also be of value to SEO team members, other marketing professionals, business leaders and anyone looking to get a better understanding of what is required to make SEO work for their business in today's world of search.

These people often have three major problem areas: **growth, trust** and **insight/knowledge:**

- They're struggling to grow their website traffic.

- They don't know who to trust to help them and may even have wasted money on substandard services in the past.

- They don't necessarily understand what the issues are, what needs doing or what the best strategy is. They also hate being drowned in technical jargon and fancy buzzwords.

The big question is: how do you get results from your SEO activity? I'll show you why you need to invest in SEO, what you need to do to get results, and who should be doing it within (or outside) your organisation.

Why you need this book

There are millions of ecommerce websites worldwide. Only a small percentage of them make any meaningful revenue. These huge numbers are misleading; it's fairly straightforward these days for anyone to launch an ecommerce store and try their luck at drop shipping or launching a product. But when it comes to online strategies, most of these failing ecommerce sites just aren't doing everything required to succeed in these competitive marketplaces.

On the other hand, those who are putting time, money and effort into their online strategies sometimes find it's just not working out for them. Does this sound like you? Is your ecommerce business performing to its full potential – or are you leaving a ton of money on the table? What's going wrong?

Read the following list of questions. How many will you answer 'yes' to:

Has your **overall** traffic seen a dip or been flatlining over the past year?

Has your organic traffic seen a dip or been flatlining over the past year?

Do you feel like you're lagging behind the competition?

Do you feel like you don't understand what SEO is?

When it comes to SEO and other acquisition channels, do you feel like you're only doing bits here and there, rather than addressing all of the important stuff?

Do you have just one or two people (or no one at all) working on SEO strategies and tactics?

Do you ever find it confusing and difficult to know what you should be doing with SEO?

Have you stopped using some of your online strategies because you worry they don't work and might be wasting your time and money?

If you answered 'Yes' to **one** of these questions – just one – this book is for you.

You'll discover what the ANCHOR model is and how it can help your SEO strategy finally take hold and lift your ecommerce business to new levels. Although this book is mainly focused on SEO, you'll also learn about the complementary channels that best support SEO and how to make the most of these. You'll learn how to combine all the strategies together, and you'll find out who is the best person to do this for your business.

How to use this book

The majority of this book will be easy to follow for anyone with a basic understanding of online marketing. There may be some sections, such as the Audit section, where I mention terms such as canonical tags and robots.txt files. If you know what I'm talking about, then that's great – crack on! But if some of the terms are unfamiliar or confusing, don't worry. It's still worth reading those parts and by reading these sections, some of the terms may become a little clearer just from the context (there is also a glossary at the end of the book which will help explain many of the terms mentioned). The book still arms you with the right questions to ask, whether that be to your developers, your in-house marketing team or your agency. You'll still get a lot of value from the rest of the book too.

I'm also happy to answer any quick questions you may have. If anything is unclear, just pop me an email at martin@wildsprout.digital or grab me if you see me at an industry event. I'm very approachable after my first coffee!

I hope you enjoy *The Organic Advantage*.

PART ONE
Why?

'SEO is Dead.'

You may well have heard this phrase from time to time; even people in the SEO industry bounce it around as bit of a joke. Would they be throwing this statement around if it were true? I'm going to get straight to the point: it's a load of bulls**t.

It isn't dead; it's just changed.

And it will continue to change.

Does SEO work?

In a fast-moving digital world, it's undeniable that SEO is very different to the way it used to be (we'll get to that shortly), but as long as there are search engines and as long as you have other businesses to compete with, then there will be SEO, there will be a need for a list and there will most certainly be paid channels. And those paid channels will continue to get more expensive, making the need for a good SEO strategy more essential than ever.

Why are more and more ecommerce business owners worrying about whether SEO is right for them – and whether it works at all? Most of the time, it's because they've tried it – either using in-house resources or by outsourcing it – and they've seen no results or, worse still, they've seen declines.

I see this time and time again, and what's the common factor when I look into the reasons? Terrible strategies and tactics. Just days before writing this book, I was approached by someone (now a client) who said they'd had someone 'doing SEO' for them over the last couple of years but they weren't seeing any results. One of the great things about this industry is that there are some great tools out there that make it easy to get a good idea of organic performance over time for almost any website. I'm talking about tools like Ahrefs and SEMrush, which are great online marketing tools. I happened to be using Ahrefs that day and popped this person's site into their Site Explorer. The number of links and referring domains was going up on a monthly basis but both the estimated traffic and the number of ranking keywords were falling steadily. Digging into those links a little deeper showed why none of the activity was working: blog comments (not good ones) and social bookmarking were the only activities taking place. Those things worked ten years ago, but if they are all you're doing today you're most certainly not going to be seeing the increases you want and need from your website.

Some people will use tactics like this because then they can write reports that say, 'Look, I've done all this over the last month.' But they're a waste of time.

Yes, SEO works – when it's done right.

GET IT RIGHT OR RISK FAILURE

One migration I worked on was for a site that had around ten million indexed pages; a large site that had millions of sessions per month. The migration was a long project and a lot was changing, for the better:

- The site structure was being overhauled.

- The site used a lot of faceted navigation and had a crazy amount of filter combinations, so crawl efficiency was being improved.

- The URL structure was changing and the redirects had to be spot on.

- The design was changing and a lot of UX would be different.

There was a huge list of things that were changing, considerations to be made, and things that it was vital to get right or risk failure.

The organic traffic of that site at the time was down 5% year on year. Within 3–6 months of the migration, that had changed to being up around 25% year on year.

This is just one example of how thinking about SEO and getting it right can make a huge difference to a business.

Whether it's a migration or an ongoing search campaign, getting SEO right is key to driving your business forward. If you look at the competition in your space and think about who you would consider to be the market leaders, you'll find that they're not there because they ignored their organic traffic channel. They're there because they work on all vital channels and improve constantly. They work on their SEO strategy (whether it's in-house or outsourced), they have a paid strategy, they're building a strong list and they're doing email marketing. They may even be on Amazon and have separate optimisation and paid strategies for that platform.

What they're not doing is saying things like, 'let's just put all our money into paid, because it's more measurable,' or, 'let's just do email marketing to our current list because it's a cheap channel that currently gives us a return.'

The channels I've just mentioned are all important, but they all have something important in common: they need to be done right.

Then and now

I doubt that you are looking for a history lesson, but it's definitely worth knowing a little about how search has changed over recent years. (For those who know this already, this would be a good opportunity to maybe just refresh your thinking and make sure you're not still doing any of the old hat stuff you probably should have stopped ten years ago.)

Then

I'm not going to go into too much fine detail of Google's Panda and Penguin updates; briefly, they were updates that Google released (in 2011 and 2012 respectively) that changed the game completely. Panda was designed mostly around site and content quality, user experience, duplicate content and so on. Penguin was introduced to tackle link spam.

Before Panda was released, search results were very different to the way they look now. They were riddled with output from content farms, duplicate content and spammy content, with so many Adsense ads above the fold that you'd do well to find the actual content you were looking for. Panda hit these sites hard and at first, the update was scary for a lot of people. But not only have the search results improved but people's approach to content and quality has changed dramatically since then. Panda was a good thing for search results and those using them.

Then around a year later, along came Penguin. I was working with an agency at the time and I remember seeing a number of other agencies using blog networks. I'm not talking about private blog networks (PBNs) that, when done well, can still work today (not that I'm advising it); I'm talking about public networks that anyone could use, sites that were all interlinked to power each other. Let's put it this way: it wasn't hard for Google to pick them out. Let's be honest here. I was so tempted to follow suit, to head down this risky road myself, due to the results people were getting. The MD of the agency said, 'It's your call, Martin.' No pressure then. But I decided that this strategy would not be in keeping with the agency's image/promise and I opted not to pursue it. And boy, am I glad I did. This update hit just as hard as Panda, if not harder.

It wasn't just the sites using spammy links and networks that were hit hard. At this point and over time, anchor text became more and more important. Once upon a time, you could hammer a page using an exact match keyword as the anchor text; today, this would land you in hot water. Thinking about anchor text usage and being careful not to over-optimise is vitally important when planning links.

Perhaps it would once have been a valid tactic to order 300 social bookmarks, syndicate some content out to multiple article sites, write an article and manually spin each sentence so that you had hundreds, if not thousands, of different versions of that same article, then syndicate that out to a network of sites, and many more equally suspect tactics... all with the same anchor text. That type of SEO is certainly dead.

Google made all these changes for the right reasons: to improve the quality of their search results in pursuit of their goal to be the best search engine available so they could dominate the market. Did they eradicate all poor content from their search results? No. Did all spammy link building tactics become useless? No. But Google made a giant leap towards those goals and these two updates completely changed the way people approach SEO today.

I say that – but it's not universally true, and herein lies part of the problem. It didn't completely change the way people work. I still regularly come across 'cheap' suppliers offering out-of-date services. I've seen their applications first-hand. They often look like this:

Dear sir,

I use only white hat tactics. I will do the following for you every month.

Article submissions

Article spinning

Social bookmark submissions

Web 2.0 sites

IFTTT syndication

Blog comments

Forum comments

Classified ad submissions

This sort of stuff wasn't white hat in 2010, it certainly isn't now, and offering these kinds of services is unfair on those who don't really understand how they all work. Please steer clear of these types of tactics.

Even the old on-page tactics (eg keyword stuffing, over-optimised title tags) are still attempted from time to time, although decreasingly so. At the time of writing this book, I was even asked to look at a site that had a load of internal links hidden in the footer. This was likely something that had been done years ago and forgotten about – but tactics like that can hurt your traffic if you're not careful.

Times have changed and if people want their businesses to grow online, their strategies and tactics need to change too. I even see people from black hat communities moving to more white hat methods.

And yes: SEO is harder these days. You can't just spin an article into 1,000 different versions and syndicate it out to 1,000 sites, then sit back and watch your rankings increase. But you know what? SEO still works! And when it's done right, it works well. Is it a quick fix that'll see you overtaking the competition in the next three months? Of course not. It takes time. But are you just looking to grow your business over the next three months and then bail out, or are you in it for the long haul?

Now

So what does SEO look like these days?

I'll tell you now: it's not just 'build great content and people will find it', as some people would have you believe. There's a lot more to driving organic traffic to a website. Great content is just one element of that and we'll come back to that aspect later.

To break it down simply, I always say to people there are two main elements to SEO: on-site and off-site. 'On-site' means the elements required to get your website in optimal order. Is your site structure as good as it can be? Your URL structure? Title tags? Content? Internal linking? Site speed? Technical SEO and on-page optimisation are really important; I often see huge gains just from fixing a lot of this stuff and getting the website right, even before getting to the off-site aspects.

The off-site elements are things like backlinks and mentions of your brand on the web. Are links still important? Absolutely. Links are still a huge ranking factor and that seems likely to continue for some time. Links are what makes the internet the internet, and they're the best way for search engines to judge the popularity and authority of one article against another. In 2014, former Google engineer Matt Cutts said that Google had experimented internally with a version of Google that didn't use links and that 'the quality looks much, much worse'. He also stated that links were 'still a really really big win in terms of quality for search results'.[1]

For the most part, this is still the case, although Google has become much better at ignoring links these days; some of your links that you think look OK may well be ignored by the big G.

We'll dig more into what you should be doing and what works later in this book but first let's look at some examples of good, bad and downright ugly campaigns.

The good, the bad and the downright ugly

Whether it's an audit, an ongoing campaign or a big migration, there are so many elements to SEO and the role is ever-changing. Strategies and tactics change as search engines do, and people in SEO roles need to be doing more to get results.

Sometimes SEO campaigns go really well, and sometimes they don't. When they fail, there are normally

---

1   M. Cutts, 'Is there a version of Google that excludes backlinks as a ranking factor?' (YouTube, 2014) www.youtube.com/watch?v= NCY3oWhI2og

good reasons for the failure. Let's look at some examples of good and bad campaigns and projects I've seen first-hand.

The good

The ANCHOR model talks about covering the necessary elements of an online strategy, and it makes up the bulk of this book. But for now, I'm just going to show you an example of this model in operation.

THE ANCHOR MODEL AT WORK

I started working with a new client about eight months before writing this book and my work with them was a classic example of the ANCHOR model in practice. You'll learn more about the details later but here's a rough breakdown of what we did.

The problem: This client had experienced a bad migration almost a year earlier. They had done all they could to try to fix things and recover but had only seen slight improvements.

The solution: The work all started, as it usually does, with the audit. And the audit revealed a lot of issues. The client's site structure and click depth were pretty poor, they had crawl efficiency issues, a lot of orphaned pages and a number of other issues, including a lot of poor-quality backlinks. After we ran through the audit, their team were great at implementing changes and the benefits of those fixes started to show quickly. As well as technical changes and implementations, there was also a lot of work around on-page optimisation, content improvements, content merges and content removal. A full backlink audit was also carried out and a disavow file submitted to Google. After these and a number of other things were done, the next phase was outreach and link building. The site already had some great content, so as well as gradually adding to this, a lot of the focus for content went into improving what was already there. With the content assets in place, outreach could begin. The site began to get a good steady stream of links even though technical and on-page improvements were still taking place. Even today, the campaign is regularly reviewed, opportunities are revealed, and work to improve things further is ongoing. Around seven months into the campaign, the site is already experiencing around 100% year on year growth and a 40% uplift in goal completions.

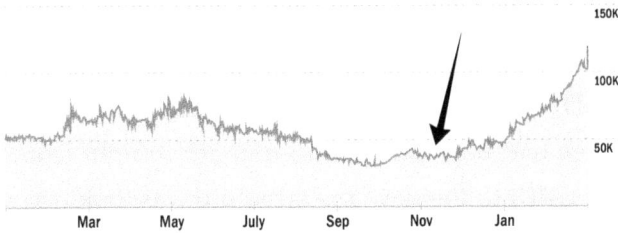

Figure 1.1 *Effect of ANCHOR implementation on site performance*

The above graph (compiled using public data from Ahrefs rather than sharing client data) shows the difference it made. The arrow shows the point at which the audit was completed and work began. You can see where the business was falling already, even before it was hurt by a problematic migration.

Things are now better than ever and they have recently been experiencing the highest traffic levels and goal conversions they've ever seen.

The bad

When migrations go wrong, they can really go wrong. I was managing a team within an agency some years ago and a client was insisting on doing their migration a few weeks before Christmas – their peak time. Despite the team advising against this plan, the client was determined to push ahead. Everything from our end was handled correctly. The structure was changing and the site was switching from a .co.uk top-level domain (TLD) to a .com. The redirects were spot on, the developers had been advised to redirect straight from the old URLs to the new, the structure was looking good. Nothing could go wrong.

Traffic fell off a cliff. Why? Because the redirects hadn't been implemented as we'd asked. They had gone something like this: Domain.co.uk/old-structure – Redirecting to Domain.co.uk/new-structure – Then redirecting to Domain.com/new-structure.

This was the dreaded redirect chain. It has never been a good thing, but we spotted this one fairly quickly and advised them accordingly. I think the client's development agency not understanding SEO was a big issue. We chased them. Then chased again. Then chased some more. Ten days later, they had fixed it, but their traffic didn't instantly reappear. We weren't expecting it to.

I think web development agencies are better these days and they at least try to have some understanding of SEO and the implications of flawed redirect implementation. But back then, not so much.

Although the team did nothing wrong in this case, we did all learn from the experience. Lessons such as:

- Test, test, test.

- Have a roll-back plan.

- Make all instructions clear enough for a five-year-old to understand, then dumb it down some more. And then double-check that everyone is on the same page.

I have done a lot of hugely successful migrations since then and love working on big ones – but perhaps some of that success is down to the experience of this not-so-glowing one.

The bad, part two

As the last example was related to a poor migration, I'd like to squeeze in one more, this time related to poor ongoing activity. This example just shows how easy it is for a so-called SEO expert to make it look like they're doing plenty of work, yet even after twelve months, organic traffic was down around 20% and the number of keywords the site was ranking for was still falling.

This was the example I mentioned earlier where links were being built on a monthly basis, but they were all poor-quality blog comments and social bookmarking links. Trust me, that approach is not going to shift the needle. I recently started working with this business and have completed the audit. The fact that I've found so many issues is good in terms of the opportunities to improve but bad in that I have to question what the other guy was ever doing.

The downright ugly

You might have heard this example before, as the events took place some years ago. The American department store chain JC Penney was penalised by Google back in 2011 but it's still worth a mention due to the size of the site and the impact it had, as well as the publicity it attracted. The company was accused of using black hat techniques and buying links, perhaps due to its SEO agency buying into some form of link network? They quickly sacked the SEO agency and managed to resolve the issues, getting the penalty lifted three months later. Even so, three months is a long time for a business of that size not to be showing in the search rankings; you can imagine the impact it had on their revenue. Although this is an old example, it just goes to show that you have to be careful when it comes to the tactics your staff or your outsourced team are using; and please avoid using the cheap services I mentioned in the last section.

PART TWO

What?

In this job, you get to see plenty of examples of people doing great work, people doing terrible work and people just not having a clue where to start. But one thing I see often is people either doing nothing or focusing down on one area and neglecting a lot of other essential stuff.

For example, they may nail the content creation but never promote the content. They may be doing some great link building but they haven't done a proper audit and the website is technically awful. Or they have a one-month burst of activity and then do little else for the rest of the year.

I've even come across marketers and business owners who are actively implementing online strategies but have no idea what the results look like.

Sometimes this is due to a lack of time or a lack of resources and support; sometimes it's down to a lack of knowledge of what to do, when and how often. And that lack of knowledge is understandable. The game of search is constantly changing and if you're not always in it, it's hard to be 'on it'.

The ANCHOR model

I devised the ANCHOR model to simplify online marketing and to act as a guide for what should be involved as part of an online strategy.

One of my clients, Mike, nailed it when he said that doing just one of the elements would be 'like going to the gym five days a week but only doing biceps'. (He loves his fitness analogies and I think he summed it up perfectly with this one.)

What is the ANCHOR model?

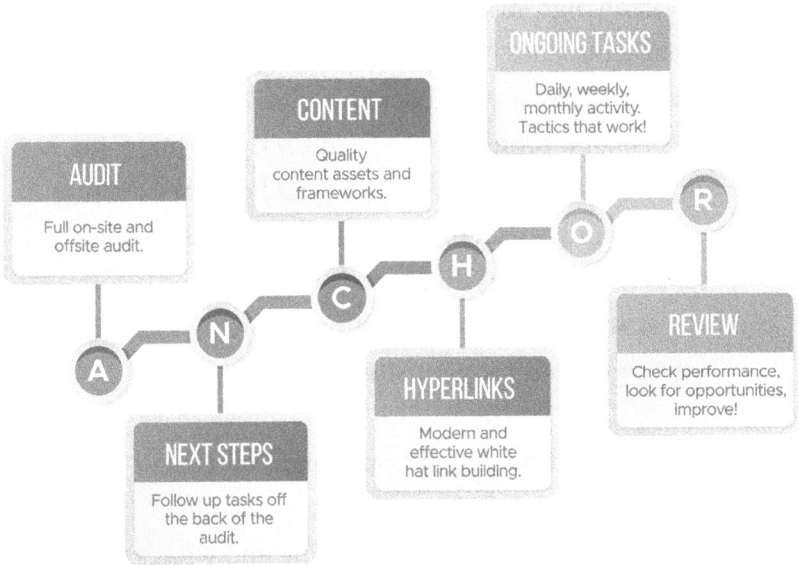

Figure 2.1 *The ANCHOR model*

ANCHOR was originally created for SEO campaigns, but it can be just as relevant for other online strategies. It breaks a campaign down into six key areas, introduced below and discussed in more detail later in this section. The six areas are:

Audit

Every campaign should start with an audit to identify the problems. Sites with great on-site optimisation can be held back by a poor backlink profile; sites with a great backlink profile can be held back by a poor site. From site crawls, structural audits and on-page analysis to keyword research, content auditing and backlink profile analysis, everything needs to be checked before changes are made. You want to make sure the changes are the right ones for your site.

This also rings true for paid campaigns and email marketing strategies. What's currently being done? How is everything set up? What's working and what's not? What can be improved straight away? What can be tested? And so on. This is the purpose of the audit stage.

Next steps

Which brings us onto the next steps. Once the audit has been completed, what are the follow-up tasks off the back of it? What technical issues need fixing? What on-page optimisation needs to be implemented? Is a backlink clean-up required? Do the paid campaigns need a complete overhaul? Do you need to set up automatic emails for customers who've abandoned purchases in their basket?

Content

Once the house is in order, it's on to content. What content assets are already in place and what needs to be created? There may be a number of directions to take. Content can be something as simple as a high-quality article, or as complex as an interactive video.

This part of the process can also relate to email marketing and paid ad content.

Hyperlinks

Links are still one of the most important, if not the most important, ranking factor, yet still so many people get this wrong. Some build poor-quality links, putting the business at risk of penalties. Some create great content and then don't market it at all – so they don't acquire any links. And some hold themselves back by just sticking to one or two tactics, due to a lack of time or resources, a limited budget, or a knowledge gap.

Links are important to a successful SEO campaign, but doing them the right way is even more important.

Link building is no longer a simple case of directory submissions, social bookmarking and forum commenting for links etc. For a link building campaign to be successful, it is essential to engage with the right people, to create great, shareable content, and to market it in the right ways.

Ongoing work

It's important to have structures in place for regular checks and ongoing tasks to be carried out on a monthly, weekly or even daily basis. These tasks range from content creation and link building to regular crawls, site checks and on-site improvements.

SEO is not a one-off job. It is not a quick fix. SEO is largely about constantly tweaking and fine-tuning, and it takes time.

MARGINAL GAINS: A SEISMIC SHIFT IN BRITISH CYCLING

In his book *Atomic Habits*, James Clear talks about 'marginal gains' in relation to the British cycling team.[1] In 2003, British professional cycling's governing body hired a new performance director, Dave Brailsford. At the time, British cyclists had endured nearly one hundred years of mediocrity, winning just one gold medal at the Olympic Games and achieving zero wins in a century of the Tour de France.

Brailsford believed the best way to win was through constant improvement and he believed in marginal gains. For him, that meant optimising by 1% wherever they could find an opportunity. He improved uniforms, sleep, diet, bikes, travel schedules. Every little thing he could optimise, he did.

Brailsford said, 'The whole principle came from the idea that if you broke down everything you could think of that goes into riding a bike, and then

---

1   J. Clear, *Atomic Habits: An Easy and Proven Way to Build Good Habits and Break Bad Ones* (Random House Business, 2018).

improve it by 1%, you will get a significant increase when you put them all together.'[2]

Brailsford and his team made the sorts of small adjustments you might expect of a cycling team – redesigning the bikes, making them more comfortable – as well as some less obvious ones like rubbing alcohol on the tyres for a better grip and providing riders with electrically heated overshorts to maintain ideal muscle temperature. They tested various fabrics in a wind tunnel and had their outdoor riders switch to indoor racing suits. And why stop there? They tested massage gels for recovery, they chose specific mattresses and pillows to ensure riders got a good night's sleep. They painted the inside of the truck white to make it easier to keep clean and minimise the risk of dust degrading the bikes' performance.

They made a huge number of small adjustments, all with the goal of finding tiny 1% gains wherever they could.

And it worked wonders. Just five years in and they were dominating. They won 60% of the gold medals

2   M. Slater, 'Olympic cycling: Marginal gains underpin Team GB dominance' (BBC Sport, 2012) https://www.bbc.co.uk/sport /olympics/19174302

available at the 2008 Olympics in Beijing and then set nine Olympic records and seven world records at the London 2012 Olympics. They also won five out of the six Tour de France races between 2012 and 2017, after winning none before the arrival of Brailsford. In that same period, British cyclists won 178 world championships, sixty-six Olympic and Paralympic gold medals and five Tours de France.

Imagine if they hadn't hired Brailsford and made all those tiny adjustments. Imagine if they had been impatient and fired him a year in because they weren't seeing results. Imagine if Brailsford hadn't been as thorough in his pursuit of marginal gains and had only implemented a few of the hundreds of changes he made.

Small changes won't do much individually but over time, all of the adjustments together can be game-changing. It's the same with SEO, paid campaigns and email marketing.

Review

Last but not least, it's important to review performance regularly. This isn't just about running a report and showing the results for the previous month; it's also about looking for opportunities to improve.

Now that we've broken down the ANCHOR model, let's dig into each of the aspects in more detail.

Audit

It's not easy to explain exactly how to carry out an audit. Every site is different. Most of the time they're structured differently and they have different issues, different opportunities, different content and different backlink profiles. The more sites you audit, the more you get an eye for things to check and look out for.

But there are some common checks and tasks that should be carried out for all sites. Some of these won't be important for all sites but they should all be checked. Although you should always be on the lookout for other issues and opportunities during this process (much of that just comes with experience), the following is a checklist for any audits you carry out:

Casting an eye/browsing

It sounds simple and not very technical, but the best place to start is by just having a good browse around the site. I like to have a notepad next to me so I can jot down any issues I come across, to remind me later.

Get a feel for the site. Consider things like:

• Does the navigation make sense and make the site easy to browse?

• How does the site feel in general from a user point of view?

• How easy is it to find the products you're looking for?

• Are there any obvious technical issues?

• Is the buying process a good user experience?

• Would you trust and buy from the site?

Make notes of your findings and keep them for later.

The crawl

Crawling a site is usually where you'll get the most insight. It will give you a better idea of the site structure, depth and other issues that are hard to spot from just browsing. When it comes to a large ecommerce site, your crawling tool is a friendly minion who will run off and check every page for you and then report back when it's done.

There are some great crawling tools out there: Screaming Frog, Sitebulb, DeepCrawl and OnCrawl are a few of the popular ones, and I would recommend you use one of them. I used Screaming Frog for years and I still think it's great, but Sitebulb is now my go-to tool, and I love it. The insights you get (and the way it visualises them) make life so much easier for someone who regularly audits sites. I've always prided myself on my audits – people have often referred me to clients for this reason – but I feel like Sitebulb has taken them up a level. Whichever tool you choose, you will need to not only get a feel for the tool itself but also use it to do some data exports; it's worth being at least a little familiar with Excel filters and formulas.

Once you've run the crawl, it's time to start digging into the data.

Site structure and crawlability

It's always a good idea to get a quick overview of how the site structure looks, but it isn't easy to see quickly from the results of your crawling tool, regardless of which one you're using.

Enter Excel. Some people don't bother with this step but I like to see how the site is structured, how many pages are in each section etc. Having the data in Excel also makes it easier to use the Google Analytics API to pull in traffic and revenue metrics next to each page.

If you export all of your internal URLs from one of the tools I mentioned above, you can then use Excel filters on the URL column to break things out into separate tabs that will come in useful later. For instance:

- Which of the URLs contain /blog/ ?

- Which of the URLs contain /product/ ?

- Which of the URLs contain p= (pagination)?

	URL	Total Clicks	Total Impressions	Title	Title Length	Meta Description	Meta Description Length	Crawl Depth
2	https://www.yourwebsite.com/category/	2000	40000	Title Tag 1 | Brand	19	Description here	16	1
3	https://www.yourwebsite.com/category/sub-category1/	2000	40000	Title Tag 2 | Brand	19	Description here	16	2
4	https://www.yourwebsite.com/category/sub-category1/sub-sub-category1/	2000	40000	Title Tag 3 | Brand	19	Description here	16	3
5	https://www.yourwebsite.com/category/sub-category1/sub-sub-category2/	2000	40000	Title Tag 4 | Brand	19	Description here	16	3
6	https://www.yourwebsite.com/category/sub-category1/sub-sub-category3/	2000	40000	Title Tag 5 | Brand	19	Description here	16	3
7	https://www.yourwebsite.com/category/sub-category1/sub-sub-category4	2000	40000	Title Tag 6 | Brand	19	Description here	16	3
8	https://www.yourwebsite.com/category/sub-category2/	2000	40000	Title Tag 7 | Brand	19	Description here	16	2
9	https://www.yourwebsite.com/category/sub-category2/sub-sub-category1	2000	40000	Title Tag 8 | Brand	19	Description here	16	3
10	https://www.yourwebsite.com/category/sub-category2/sub-sub-category2/	2000	40000	Title Tag 8 | Brand	19	Description here	16	3
11	https://www.yourwebsite.com/category/sub-category2/sub-sub-category3	2000	40000	Title Tag 9 | Brand	19	Description here	16	3
12	https://www.yourwebsite.com/category/sub-category1/sub-sub-category9	2000	40000	Title Tag 10 | Brand	19	Description here	16	3

Full Crawl | General | Categories | Products | Brands | Packages | Blog | Pagination

Figure 2.2 Breaking down the data using Excel

Some sites might have opted for a completely flat URL structure with most pages at the same level in the hierarchy, and that makes things a little trickier. I'll talk about that more below in the 'URL structure' section, but having both categories and products in a flat structure like this is not logical for search engines, not always helpful to users, and it can make reporting, insights and auditing harder. If you're dealing with a structure like this, then there may be a little bit of manual filtering involved.

You may even be dealing with a URL structure that makes no sense at all, with URLs like www.myshop .com/465936/. Although this kind of thing is less common than it once was, it makes filtering trickier again.

Once you have your crawl sheet, your site structure will be a lot clearer. You can see how many category pages you have, how many product pages, how many blog posts. All in one quick view and in a format you can make more use of later.

In relation to site structure and crawlability, there are some other things to consider:

- How many pages do I have indexed by Google?

- How does that compare to the number of pages on my site and the number of pages I actually *want* indexed?

- Do I have 'Index Bloat'?

- Of the pages that were crawled, how many are set to noindex?

- How many are blocked by robots.txt?

- How many use canonical tags pointing to other pages?

- Are any pages indexed unnecessarily? What pages are just wasting 'crawl budget'?

- How many internal links use the 'nofollow' attribute?

Everyone has different levels of knowledge and to some, many of the points above won't make much sense. But whether you understand them or not, they are all things that need to be considered and checked as you audit your site.

Crawl depth

When I talk about crawl depth, I mean the number of clicks it takes to get to the required page. It's important because the deeper your pages are, the less likely they are to be crawled and indexed by search engines. Put it this way: if a page is ten levels deep from the homepage, why would a search engine deem it as worth ranking? It can't be that important to your business if you've buried it ten levels deep, right?

Ideally, most of your site should be accessible within three to four clicks, but I'm not advocating cramming links to every single page onto your homepage. The site structure still needs to be logical and user-friendly. For example, you might link to your categories in the main navigation and then to your products from those, as is the case with most ecommerce sites. But if you have categories, sub-categories, sub-sub-categories, five products per page and a huge amount of pagination with only three clickable pages at a time, many of your products are likely to be buried too deep in the structure.

I've worked with many businesses who started out with very high crawl depths. For example, they may have had a huge spike in pages at around level 6–8. If you find something like this, it could be an issue and should always be looked into further.

URL structure

URL structure is different from site structure. As mentioned in the 'Site structure and crawlability' section, sometimes a site has a good, clean logical URL structure. Some sites have a completely flat structure such as:

www.myshop.com/about-us/ (page)

www.myshop.com/dresses/ (category)

www.myshop.com/flower-maxi-dress/ (product)

Some even have a nonsensical structure with no keywords: www.myshop.com/465936/.

Although URL structure is only a tiny ranking factor, it's these small things working together that make sites optimal – back to the marginal gains. So, having a logical URL structure matters to your business and using keywords without being spammy is also important.

But this isn't the time to just go changing your URLs. You'll need to properly redirect the current URLs to the new ones, and you need to be careful when it comes to anything URL-related, or chaos can result.

Robots.txt

All sites should have a robots.txt file. This file sits on the root of your site and tells search engines what pages they can and can't look at (this is especially useful for many ecommerce sites due to their size and the use of certain filters etc). This file should always be checked as part of an audit, and the checks should include these questions:

- Is there a robots.txt file in place? (It will sit here: www.myshop.com/robots.txt)

- Is it blocking anything it shouldn't be?

- Are there things that should be blocked but aren't?

XML sitemaps

An XML sitemap is an additional way for search engines to find and index all of your pages. It's good to check this for quality by asking questions like:

- Is an XML sitemap in place?

- Has it been submitted to Google Search Console?

- Are there any broken URLs in the sitemap?

- Are there any URLs that go through redirects in the sitemap?

- Are any URLs missing from the sitemap?

- Are there pages in there that aren't accessible on the site (orphaned pages)?

Filters and parameters

I didn't want to make this book too technical so I'll only dig into a little detail here – but the use of filters and parameters is a big issue for ecommerce SEO and can sometimes be the cause of many problems. These may be in the form of manufacturer, size, or price filters, or may be related to page ordering, the number of products per page etc.

Many ecommerce platforms have some solutions in place, such as canonical tags for page ordering options, but using filters and faceted navigation isn't always straightforward. I've worked with classified sites where categories allowed you to select multiple filters;

for some time, search engines could crawl and index every single combination of filters, resulting in millions of pages. When we had the analytics team really dig into it, none of the pages beyond a combination of two filters actually drove any traffic.

When it comes to resolving this issue, there are a number of options. I can't tell you exactly how to sort this out because it depends on a number of factors, but some common solutions include: using javascript to make certain filters uncrawlable; setting some filter links to 'nofollow' and the destination pages to 'noindex'; using robots.txt; and using canonical tags.

Internal linking

Search engines crawl sites to learn about their structure, to discover new content, and to get an idea of which pages are important and which aren't. Internal linking is a big part of this and it's hugely important for SEO. It's also one of those things that the sites I come across can always improve on. But there are some important factors to consider, such as:

- Relevance – are the internal links relevant or forced in where it doesn't make sense?

- Anchor text – it's crucial to get this right and not to be too aggressive with it.

It's also a good idea to check how many times each of your pages is internally linked to and what you're prioritising (you can check this in Google Search Console). Looking at this often throws up some surprises.

Title tags

There are still some people out there who think 'doing SEO' is just a matter of tweaking a few title tags. I hope you're realising by now that it's just one factor of many to consider – but it's still an important one. These tags are an important on-page element, and should be fully optimised.

Tags should be within the recommended character limits; they should include the keyword(s) or topic relevant to that page; they should be unique to every page; and they should **not** be over-optimised – trust me, that won't help you.

There are some simple issues that can be picked up quickly using crawling tools, such as:

- Title tags that are too long

- Title tags that are too short

- Title tags that are missing

Rules can be used for things like product title tags, but much of the real optimisation will be done manually. The spreadsheet I mentioned earlier – the one we used to segment the site structure into different sections – will come in handy here. For example, you may want to prioritise working on improving the categories. There's a tab for that!

Meta descriptions

Meta descriptions are another important element. They are used within Google search results as a snippet of text to further describe any given page. Like title tags, the meta descriptions should be unique to each page; they should aim to complement the title tag in describing the page as explicitly as possible within the recommended character limits. Although they are not a ranking factor, they should aim to be compelling in their tone and try to stand out as unique, increasing the number of user click-throughs. Click-through rate can be a contributing ranking factor, so indirectly this is still important for SEO.

Header elements

Header elements, much like title tags, are HTML elements utilised by search engines to describe the purpose and content of any page. There should only be one <h1> tag per page and it should be unique in comparison to other pages on the site.

Typically, an <h1> tag should include key phrases similar to those in the title tag. Header tags should be used in a logical hierarchy. For example:

<h1>Page heading</h1>

    <h2>Section heading</h2>

        <h3>Section subheading level 1</h3>

    <h2>Section heading</h2>

        <h3>Section subheading level 1</h3>

            <h4>Section subheading level 2</h4>

<h4>Section subheading level 2</h4>

As with the title tags, be wary of over-optimisation.

Images

Images are often neglected elements of web pages. But they shouldn't be ignored – remember those marginal gains. Simply giving the image file a meaningful name (instead of calling it g456739.png) and adding an alt tag can help with relevance and can also help your site to appear in places like Google Images, or even on the main search results page, depending on the search term.

Alt tags are fairly easy to audit and they should be part of your checks.

Technical issues

A big part of doing an audit is looking for technical issues. If a site has a large number of issues, fixing them can often result in a quick win, as long as they can be fixed fairly readily. Some issues may have been discovered during the initial browse, so the notes you made will come in handy now.

Some issues might have been picked up while digging into the site structure and assessing crawlability. But don't assume that's the end of it; there can often be a sea of other issues lurking in your website. Some can be picked up by tools and some may require more digging. Issues you might find include:

- 404 error handling

- Crawl errors

- 404 broken links

- 3xx redirects

- Broken external links

- Problematic use of canonical tags and noindex

- Duplication (with other pages on the site)

- External duplication (eg using manufacturers' standard product descriptions instead of unique ones)

- Canonicalisation (eg does the non-www URL redirect to the www version?)

HTTPS

Back in 2014, Google announced that having a secure site (one using a HTTPS certificate) would be a slight advantage when it came to rankings. The way they put it back then was that, all other things being equal between two sites, the secure site would get the higher ranking. For ecommerce sites especially, having a secure site today is more important than ever.

TOP TIP

There have been more and more cases of ecommerce sites benefiting from choosing an EV (Extended Validation) SSL Certificate over cheaper alternatives. The process of obtaining an EV certificate requires identity verification, so they are harder to get and more trusted by users – and likely more trusted by Google too. The direct SEO impact of these is still debatable but they potentially help with trust for users too so there's more than one reason to consider using one.

Page speed

Page speed is another element that Google announced as a small ranking factor some time ago, and another that has become more important over time. Users have become used to fast internet speeds; these days, having a site whose speed doesn't quite match those user expectations can result in poor user metrics and lost sales. Users are a fussy bunch!

A number of tools can be used to test page speed. Here are a few recommendations:

- Lighthouse

- Google PageSpeed Insights

- WebPageTest

- GTmetrix

- Pingdom

These useful tools tend to give recommendations, too. If you're not technical, then it's time to talk to your developer about them.

Content

Yes, content has its own letter in the ANCHOR model, but it should still be part of the audit because it can still throw up a number of issues. A content audit can produce many insights into what's working and what isn't. You'll discover more about what's driving traffic and what's driving none, about what categories are performing well and which ones are never even being found. You'll also get insights into pages that are receiving traffic but performing badly and need to be improved.

This is a good moment to talk about content culls. I have been a fan of doing this for some time now and I'm not the only one seeing great results. It used to be the done thing to create pages for as many keyword variations and synonyms as possible and to just pump out content – the more the better. It may come as a surprise to you, but things are different these days. To put it simply: having a huge amount of content on your site that doesn't receive traffic and doesn't perform is just going to drown out the important parts of your site (like categories) and hold the site back in the rankings.

These days, it's not unusual to see someone delete 30% of their entire site and find an uplift of 25% in organic traffic; suddenly, Google is focusing on the important stuff, the site is more crawl efficient, and the crawlers aren't wasting time on terrible content.

Some key things to think about when it comes to your current content:

- Does it receive traffic?

- What are the user metrics like?

- What are your top performing pages/categories/products?

- What are your worst performing categories and products? Why?

- How much blog content do you have?

- How does your blog content perform?

You can go into huge depth with analysing content and the subject could be a book in itself. But it's essential to check at least some of these key elements and to reduce waste where possible.

Relevance

Google has become an extremely smart search engine over the years and has changed from being focused on keywords to understanding topics and relevance. And those things have become more important than ever. Long gone are the days when you could just squeeze keywords into a post to help it rank; it's far from that simple now. In order to rank now, content has to be highly relevant to the given topic. Google won't just look out for the keywords *you* want to rank for; it will be looking for other semantically relevant terms for that topic (I'll talk more about semantic relevance and LSI later). It's not uncommon these days for a page to rank for a term without even mentioning it exactly. Google is smart enough to know that the page is still about the thing the users are searching for.

Have a look at your content. Is it relevant enough? Does it fully cover the topic? Even for pages with less written content, like categories, are the products and content relevant to what the category is focusing on? You'd be surprised how often these elements drift into irrelevance.

UX issues

For years to come, there will be discussions around whether user experience is a ranking factor. As much as some people at Google deny some of the theories, I'm confident that some user experience factors affect rankings.

Regardless of whether it affects the rankings, user experience should still be considered when auditing a site. Some things to consider include:

- What are my click-through rates from Google? (You can use Search Console for this.)

- How long are users spending on my site? Can I improve this?

- How many users are bouncing back to search results after landing on my site? Can I improve this?

- How many of my site's pages are users visiting?

- Are people finding what they're looking for?

- Are they finding the products they want?

- Are they converting?

Mobile

Years ago, I was working at a company and got called into a meeting. I was told that one of the business's ecommerce sites was migrating to a new theme and that the site structure and URL structure would also be changing. They thought it would be good to talk about the SEO side of things… two weeks before the proposed launch date. Early in the meeting, while they were showing me the site's new look, I asked, 'How does this look on mobile?' Faces went blank. Worried looks were exchanged. No one had checked! Out popped the phones and they started checking the responsive mobile version. It was awful. It looked terrible, was dreadful from a user experience point of view… and it immediately put paid to that proposed launch date. The real kicker here was that mobile accounted for about 55–60% of their traffic.

More and more businesses are thinking 'mobile first' these days. Looking at the mobile side during an audit is essential, especially since the launch of Google's 'mobile first' index; Google now ranks sites based on their mobile version first.

There are good testing tools available, the main one being Google's Mobile-Friendly Test.

Other issues

Almost every site has different technical issues, so it's almost impossible to list everything you should be looking out for in one book. During the browse phase and the rest of the audit stage, I often make notes of these other issues. They may be quite big problems that warrant their own section in the audit documentation, or they may just be quick bullets under the 'Other issues' section – but however they're communicated, they should be added to the list of things to fix.

Schema

Schema is a type of HTML markup that can tell search engines more about elements of your site and pages. These can also then appear as 'rich results' in Google within the search results. Schema can be especially useful for ecommerce sites. For example, if you're using product schema on your product pages, you may see star reviews and price details in the Google search results for those products. This can really help your results stand out and improve click-through rates.

Be aware that it's entirely up to Google whether these rich results are displayed or not and that, other than adding the correct markup to your pages, there's little else you can do to sway the decision. I often have people saying things like, 'Hey, Martin – I'm using product schema but I'm not seeing the star ratings under my products. Why is that?' Usually the answer is that Google just doesn't show the rich results for that type of search. You never know when it might change, though, so it's always worth thinking about the type of schema you're using throughout your site.

Google Analytics

For Google Analytics, or whatever other analytics tool an organisation is using, there are different levels of user. There are experts who like to delve into everything from traffic and performance to funnels and user behaviour. There may be a variety of intermediate users who like to dig into a few specific metrics that they're used to checking, like organic traffic and revenue. And then there are those who hardly ever check it, if they check it at all; or worse still, have lost their login details or don't even have it installed.

We'll talk more about the ongoing use of Analytics in the R section of ANCHOR but during the auditing stage, there are a few key things to check:

- Is Analytics set up and working?

- Is the correct code being used and is it consistent across the whole site?

- Is the code missing from any pages?

Beyond this, it's a good idea to dive into an 'insights and opportunities' review during the audit phase. This is a great chance to look for performance issues, opportunities for quick improvements, highs and lows, conversion rate issues, comparisons of acquisition channels etc. It doesn't have to be mind-blowingly detailed (unless you want to go to that level) but it's certainly a good idea to dig around in your analytics while auditing your site.

I mentioned earlier that you can also use the Google Analytics API. With a quick bit of research, this is surprisingly easy to do using Google Sheets, even if you're not very technical. Using the spreadsheet we created as part of the crawl process, we can pull in some really useful data like organic traffic, transactions, revenue, conversion rate and so on, down to page level. And of course, this is also split out by section due to the way we built those sheets, making it easier to get a quick view of which pages and sections of the site are performing.

Google Search Console

It's surprising how many ecommerce business owners I speak to don't know what Google Search Console is, have it set up incorrectly, or don't have it set up at all. Every website should have Google Search Console. This free tool gives us access to extremely useful data about a website, ranging from details about the number of pages a site has in Google's index and how many pages in the XML sitemap are indexed, to how our site is performing. Site performance details in Search Console include impressions, clicks, average ranking data and click-through rates. It's also the only Google tool that still gives access to keyword data. All of this data can be extremely useful as part of the initial audit and also comes in handy for ongoing optimisation in the future. Search Console is good to audit initially, to review overall website health.

Backlinks

The subject of backlinks is another one of those areas that could be a book in itself. But for the purposes of this one, let's stick to the important stuff. Depending on your role in an ecommerce business, you may or may not be aware of the current state of your backlink profile. If you're unsure, or just starting to work on a site, then a backlink audit is an essential part of the overall audit process. It will not only guide part of your strategy going forward, but also highlight any potential issues such as a spammy backlink profile or over-optimised anchor text.

I find the best tools for this job are Ahrefs and Majestic as they tend to be more comprehensive.

Here are some examples of key things to look out for when performing a backlink audit:

- How many links/referring domains does the site have and what is the quality like?

- How does the anchor text distribution look?

- Are there spammy links in the profile?

- Does the link velocity look unnatural?

- Are there links going to deeper pages?

- Are there links pointing to broken pages on your site?

Keyword research

Some people might opt to do keyword research before anything else, while others may prefer to do it after the audit, once they have a better understanding of the site as a whole. You may hear people talking about keywords becoming less important and the search game being more about 'topics' today – as I discussed in the 'Relevance' section above – but it's still important to do the research within and around those topics.

I like to do a top-level keyword research view as part of the audit, looking at general terms, category level and commercial terms, initial content ideas etc. We can then start to think about page and topic level research during the ongoing work. We'll talk more about that later.

Competitors

The audit phase is also a good opportunity to dig into what your competitors are doing. Some people opt for a quick overview, researching who the competitors are, using them to help with keyword research, checking their backlink profiles etc, and some like to dig a lot deeper. However you choose to do it, it's definitely worth looking at competitors at some level. I find competitor analysis more useful later on, as you'll see later.

International sites

With the rise of multinational ecommerce businesses, international issues deserve a mention. There are many ways to go about the international side of SEO but let's keep it simple.

These sites tend to either be separate TLDs (.com, .co.uk, .de etc), subdirectories or subdomains. I often get asked which is best to go for and as with many things, it depends and there are pros and cons to these.

One thing I would insist on is making sure hreflang is implemented. I've seen many examples of international sites conflicting and causing problems for each other. I've also seen great examples of hreflang resolving these issues.

Documenting everything

Whether you're presenting your findings to the CEO or just passing some actions onto the developers, it's a good idea to document the whole audit process. This will make it easier to action, easier to explain to other people and easier to refer back to when you conduct future audits or need to look at what was recommended in the past.

Next steps

You know by now that the audit phase is not a small task and that, if done right, it can reveal some invaluable insights and opportunities. But what's the point of all that work if the resulting document then gets tossed aside like yesterday's newspaper? That's where the N of ANCHOR comes in. An audit without Next steps would be fairly useless; it's time to start putting actions into place. Fix and improve.

With so much to do and so many other priorities in the mix, businesses often find it hard implementing everything that comes out of the audit phase. Whether or not this sounds like your business, it's important to prioritise. You may find it useful to list the recommended actions by their potential impact. Then you'll need to consider timescales, costs, risks, feasibility of implementation etc. If you can implement impactful actions quickly, you're off to a good start.

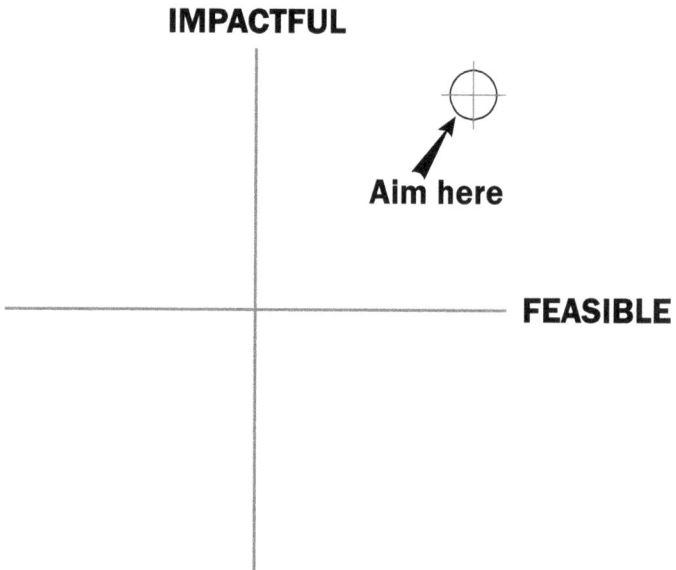

IMPACTFUL

Aim here

FEASIBLE

Figure 2.3 *Prioritising next steps*

Implementing the next steps can not only result in good initial gains but can also put the business in a strong position to proceed with ongoing future work.

MAKING THE CHANGES

In the summer of 2017, I was asked to do a one-off audit for a decent-sized ecommerce site. It was a fairly large audit, accounting for all of their global websites but with a main focus on the UK site. It rooted out a whole load of crawl efficiency issues as well as a large number of other technical SEO problems and areas for improvement. There were also endless on-page optimisation opportunities. The fixes, changes and improvements were implemented gradually over the following months and they quickly saw the benefits. Over the next six months, the business saw a year on year increase of around 40% in both organic traffic and revenue. I'm pleased to say this company is now an ongoing client.

Just as some food for thought, let's look at some examples of next steps:

- Fixing crawl errors

- Improving the site structure

- Improving crawl depth

- Improving crawlability (eg using canonicals, noindex)

- Improving the URL structure (be careful with this one: 301 redirects are needed)

- Fixing/optimising robots.txt

- Fixing sitemaps

- Improving internal linking

- Improving title tags

- Improving meta descriptions

- Improving header tags

- Adding alt text to images

- Setting up a custom 404 page

- Fixing internal redirect links

- Fixing broken internal links

- Fixing broken external links

- Sorting duplication issues

- Rewriting product descriptions

- Improving category descriptions

- Improving blog content

- Planning new blog content

Disavow

When Google released Penguin 4.0 in 2016, they said that the algorithm would run in real time from then on; rather than making the necessary improvements to your link profile and then having to wait a year until the next Penguin update, the effects would be fairly instantaneous and you could potentially see quicker recoveries. Google also said that they would ignore poor links rather than punishing sites for having them. Manual penalties would still exist, but algorithmic penalties wouldn't work in the same way.

Great! So that should be the end of negative SEO and there should no longer be a need for the disavow file, right, because Google does it automatically? Well... no, not really. There are still cases of negative SEO affecting sites and I'll talk more later about why I still use the disavow file from time to time.

The next steps that come out of the audit will be different for every site. I'd expected this section to be much longer but other than give you some advice on prioritising and some examples, there's little else to say because it can be such an open list. All I'll say is: fix as much as you can and get your house in order.

Content

Content is King!

If you've heard that a thousand times before then I'm sure you're as bored of it as I am. And if you've never heard it before, then lucky you. Like many clichés, there is some truth to it, in that content is extremely important. But what content are we talking about? Especially in the realm of ecommerce, there are various types of pages and content: categories, products, buying guides, blog posts. We will discuss all of these below.

First, I'll focus a little more on the generic use of the word 'content' and content marketing. And before we dive in and start talking about content, I just wanted to mention competitor analysis. The Content part of ANCHOR is one area where you'll find this extremely useful. If you were planning a particular type of content, some examples of how you could use competitor analysis to guide that creation are as follows:

- Look at what your competitors have created and create something that's ten times better than anything on page 1 of the search results.

- Look at the average word count on page 1 of Google for your content's focus terms. If the average word count is 3,000 then going in with 300 might not cut it.

- Look at the average anchor text distribution of the top five pages. Google treats search terms differently and it's worth checking this as a guide. If your page is heavier on exact match anchors than all of those pages, for example, you might want to dumb it down.

- Look at where they're getting their links from. We'll talk more about links later, but you might want to check this before creating the content.

- Look at how well other content has performed. Tools like BuzzSumo and Ahrefs allow you to see the performance of content in terms of social shares and/or links. You can even just search by keywords and find the top performing pages for those topics. This is a great way of finding new content ideas.

THE SKYSCRAPER TECHNIQUE

The idea of finding a piece of content that's performing well and then making something much better isn't revolutionary, but it was popularised by Brian Dean when he coined the term 'skyscraper technique'.[3] If you haven't come across his post, it's well worth a read. Put simply, Brian would find old content that had performed well and create something ten times better. He would then find the people who had linked to and shared those old pieces and reach out to them, knowing there would be a good chance of them linking to and/or sharing his new improved content as well.

Brian is a good example of someone who knows how to create amazing content. He does long-form content extremely well and his posts do a great job of earning links. He doesn't create much in terms of quantity – but he certainly understands the importance of depth and quality.

---

3   B. Dean, 'Linking Building Case Study: How I Increased My Search Traffic by 110% in 14 Days' (Backlinko, 2016) https://backlinko.com/skyscraper-technique

Content types

When it comes to creating content for ecommerce sites, there's a lot more to think about than just writing a blog. The other main elements to consider are category pages and product pages. There is no hard and fast rule for optimising your content for these – but there are some general guidelines that may help.

Category pages

There are some common questions I encounter when I discuss ecommerce category pages with clients. They include 'How many words should I have on my category page?' and 'Why does that site's category page rank when it has zero content?' As you will have realised by now, Google has a huge number of ranking factors and for us mere mortals to give exact reasons for a particular page's ranking would be nearly impossible – although with the evolution of Google's machine learning, most of the Google spam team would probably struggle with it too now. But we have an idea of how it works from years of testing and staring at the search results.

Some sites have highly ranked categories with no written content on the page – just products. And you'll usually find that these sites are brands with good authority.
Google doesn't rely purely on content to determine
what a page is about. If a site has built a huge brand and
link profile and is talked about a lot online, Google will
recognise that. The site may have great internal linking
to those category pages with descriptive anchor text
and relevant context; Google will see it. It may have
well-optimised title tags and header tags; Google will
see them. They may have good-quality and relevant
backlinks to that particular category; Google will notice
them. Depending on where you are in relation to the
competition, you may need some content on the page
to help with relevance. You may find it gives you an
edge. It could be a chance to help with cross-linking
between relevant pages and categories. And it might
be useful to your users to be able to read more about
a category and what you offer. But there isn't a hard
and fast rule like 'you should always add 300 words
of content to your category page'. The best advice I
can give is to look at what the rest of the companies
on page 1 are doing and to test, test, test.

But you should also remember that category pages are
likely to be the ones with the biggest search volumes
and are likely to be your biggest drivers of traffic to

individual pages. Be sure to give your category pages the time and attention they deserve. Think about any content that's on there and optimise it. Think about internal linking. Think about backlinks. Think about supporting content and relevance. Think about marginal gains.

Product pages

Individual product pages will rarely be the ones that bring in huge amounts of traffic by themselves – but when there are lots of products available on a site, that traffic can often mount up. You may have some products that perform well in search and some that get no natural traffic at all. Total that traffic up, and you may find it contributes a decent percentage of the site's organic traffic. But sitting down and individually optimising thousands of product pages is probably unrealistic, unless you have a lot of spare time on your hands. So what can you do to optimise them?

First of all, I want to talk about something I touched on in the 'Technical issues' section of the Audit phase, relating to manufacturer descriptions. If all your product pages are just using standard manufacturer descriptions, you're using the same text as tons of other sites and you're unlikely ever to rank these pages. In which case, you're missing a trick. There have been numerous case studies where businesses have rewritten all of their manufacturers' descriptions to make them unique, useful and compelling. Was it a huge amount of work? Of course. But did they get results? Yes. They saw significant uplifts in traffic.

If you have a lot of products, doing this across all of them might be unrealistic – but you have analytics data, remember? You can prioritise your top performing products and then set processes in place for any new product additions to be rewritten before they go live on the site. And when I say 'rewritten', I don't just mean a little 'spinning' and using a few synonyms here and there; I mean writing the content as if you were doing it from scratch and really wanted to sell the product to the customer.

Here are a few things to consider when you're writing product descriptions:

- Make sure they're highly relevant to that specific product.

- Talk about the benefits of the product and remember that any user reading it is a potential customer; you're trying to sell this product to them.

- If you have a lot of similar products, be sure to differentiate them. Something must make each one different, or you wouldn't have separate pages, right? For example, if you have separate pages for different sizes of the same product, then maybe they could all be on one product page with a drop-down selection for size. If not, perhaps they could use canonical tags to make one of the pages the preferred version to show users in search results.

- Make sure all pages are optimised differently and are targeting different keywords. As with the point above, if pages are too similar and conflict with each other, there's a good chance they'll conflict in Google's eyes too. The usual result of this is that they end up dragging each other down in the rankings. Tools like Pi Datametrics are great for picking up cannibalisation like this. Ahrefs also has a cannibalisation feature but you have to look at it on a keyword-by-keyword basis. If you don't have budget for tools like this, then you'll just have to use some common sense and make sure each of your pages is as unique as possible.

- Make sure you have breadcrumbs on your product pages, linking back to sub-category and category levels. This can be useful for both users and search engines.

Content, content, content

When it comes to general content, there are various types and frameworks you can use and the choice often depends on the purpose of the content. Here are some examples of what I mean by 'purpose':

- General supporting content – this may be present to help users but may also help with relevance. If you have a large site with only one page about a certain topic, it may struggle to rank, whereas a site with lots of relevance around that topic, and linking to it, will be in a much better place.

- Content for links – I don't believe in the 'build great content and the links will come' approach. Some people create great, linkable content assets in the hope that they will 'earn' links, but marketing is essential. You still have to promote your content.

- Content for shares – shares and links will often come hand in hand, but some content may be created specifically with brand exposure in mind. It might not get tons of links but if it gets a huge number of shares and lots of exposure, that's still a good thing.

- Content for ranking – this may go hand in hand with some of the above considerations, but some content is created with the sales funnel in mind. For example, when potential customers are in the consideration phase, it often makes sense to try and rank content that may help to sway them towards a purchase: a buying guide, a 'best of' guide, a product review or a how-to guide on using a particular item.

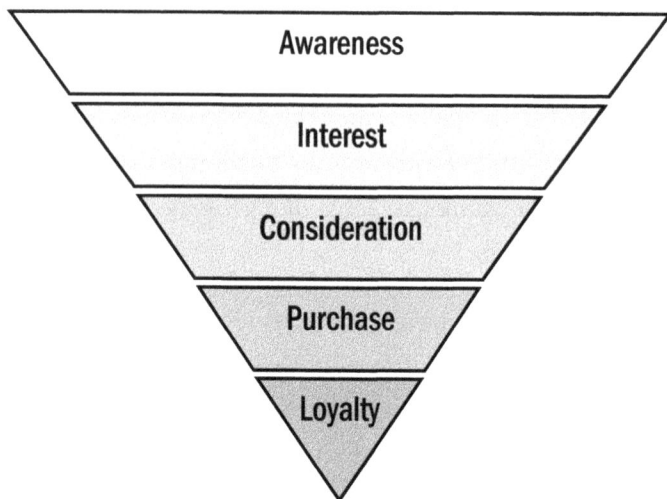

Figure 2.4 *The sales funnel*

Frameworks

When you design new content, you should be long past writing a quick 500-word post, calling it an 'Ultimate Guide' and then expecting it to do well. Quality is more important than ever and there are a handful of frameworks that are particularly effective at gaining links, shares, exposure and organic traffic.

List posts

The old way – and still the most common way – of doing list posts was to write about, say, the top ten tips on a chosen subject and then write a short blurb about each. More often than not, this was extremely unhelpful and even if there were some decent tips lurking in there, the user would have to go elsewhere to find out how to actually do them. Well-written list posts nowadays are more thorough and cover the topic in depth. Each point is often like a mini-post in itself and the user shouldn't need to go elsewhere.

Guides

Guides can often be similar to list posts, but a guide is usually more of a step-by-step 'How-To' piece rather than a series of numbered points. The length of a guide post depends on how long it takes to cover the given topic in depth, but it could be anything from 1,000 to 15,000 words.

Ego bait

People love having their egos rubbed. Human nature says that if someone is featured in a Top 50 list within their industry, they're more likely to share or even link to the post. You don't have to ask specifically for links – in fact, Google don't like it if you do – but you can let the featured people know that they're welcome to share with their audience. Often the links will follow naturally. But remember also to make sure the post is useful to your readers. If you post this kind of content only for the sake of shares and links, the quality is likely to dip.

Expert roundups

These are another great way of rubbing egos – but this time you don't even have to write your own content. Reach out to influencers in your industry and ask them a question; something that, once answered, should provide your users with real value. And don't be shy with it. The more experts, the more value – and the better your post. Who wouldn't want to share their wisdom with the masses when they've just been recognised as an expert?

Infographics and other rich media

I hear some of you saying, 'Infographics are so yesterday!' Maybe so, but they still have their place. If there's a compelling message, people still love to link to and share something visual. And if you can get creative with things like interactive infographics, then even better. We're visual creatures, which is why infographics, images and video perform so well. Video especially is growing rapidly and if you're still avoiding it, it really is time to jump on board.

Content ideas

There are many techniques for finding content ideas and adding them to your content calendar; I just want to talk about a few examples in the hope that they might inspire you. Running out of ideas is a content marketer's nightmare and it's always good to have some other general ideas under your belt. Although I've already mentioned some strong frameworks, here are some more examples:

- Interviews
- Product reviews
- Comparison posts
- Research-based content
- Case studies
- Survey-based content
- Quizzes
- Roundup posts

- Cheat sheets

- Checklists

Topic/page level keyword research

'Forget about keywords – think about topics.' I hear this more and more these days and there is some truth to it. You shouldn't be writing different pieces of content for each keyword variation anymore; Google is much smarter than it was at understanding the relationships between connected terms, so doing that will be more likely to cause cannibalisation/conflict than to help your site. Instead, you should be thinking more about creating your content around a topic.

Does that mean forgetting keywords entirely? No.

There is still huge value in doing keyword research for a topic to ensure you're talking about the right things, covering all elements of that topic, prioritising what you talk about based on search volumes, and so on.

It's also worth tracking some of these. I always tell people to forget about the rankings of an individual keyword. Would you rather rank for one vanity term and not care about anything else, or rank a page for thousands of different terms that continue to drive increasing organic traffic over time? Even in the pre-Penguin days, I started working with a client who wanted to rank a page for one term. He didn't care about anything else – even when I pointed out the huge increase in organic traffic and the other 11,000 keywords that were driving it. Even today I get asked about setting key performance indicators around keyword rankings, and I refuse. We're way past focusing on individual keywords. Let's focus on the important stuff: driving more traffic and revenue.

Semantic search and LSI

As I've already mentioned, Google is smart and getting smarter by the day. Thanks to its introduction of things like Hummingbird, RankBrain and machine learning, relevance has become perhaps the most important word in SEO today. Google has become incredibly efficient at determining user intent during a search, as well as understanding the relevance of different pages, to surface the best content (most of the time, anyway).

Although it makes things harder than simply stuffing your content with keywords and watching it rank, there are still ways you can help your content with all this in mind. If you've heard of Latent Semantic Indexing (LSI) and TF*IDF then that's great. I'm not going to go into massive detail here because it gets complicated but if you haven't heard of them, here's a simple explanation. In very basic terms, TF*IDF is a weighting score related to term usage. And using relevant LSI terms can help with document relevance.

I've read a few posts that seem to refer to LSI terms as 'synonyms'. If you've ever heard this, let me correct that impression now. These are not synonyms – they are semantically relevant terms. An example I like to give to explain the difference is my 'Donald Trump' analogy. Let's say you want to rank a page for 'Donald Trump'. You've created a page and it mentions Donald Trump – but how does Google know that your page is actually about Donald Trump and not just mentioning him in passing? Relevance. And that's where the LSI terms come in. Google is expecting to see words and phrases like 'President', 'White House', and 'The Apprentice'. See what I mean? Those aren't synonyms, they're LSI terms.

How much? How often?

You could ask a dozen experts these questions and easily get different answers from each of them. Some people will create one big piece of content every few months, but they'll make sure it's epic and gets the attention it deserves. Some will post daily and use the 'see what works' approach. Most will fall in between these two extremes. Going for quality but not posting very often can work – but you really do need to ensure the content is great and that you make the most of it. On the other hand, producing more regular content can be a good way to go as long as you're still aiming for quality and you keep on top of what's already been done.

Let me elaborate. Imagine that you've done your research and now you have a huge list of great content ideas. You have a team of writers at the ready and you start pushing out regular content. If 95% of that content doesn't perform, you'll end up with a site that gets bigger and bigger but with 95% of the content being a complete waste of time. (Remember what we said during the content auditing stage about reducing waste?) If you're taking this approach, be sure to keep on top of your analytics. Consider the following:

- What content has been live for a few months but isn't driving any traffic?

- Is it ranking for anything (use tools like SEMrush and Ahrefs)?

- Could I improve the content and/or expand on it (use Google Search Console to see what terms the page is showing for and consider expanding the content based on these)?

- Does this content conflict with another page? Should I merge them?

- Should I just cut the waste and remove it?

And if content is performing, don't stop there. Ask yourself whether you can expand on and/or improve it further. Could you utilise internal linking to help pages further? Those are the kind of things you should be considering.

Deciding how much content to produce often comes down to budget. Sometimes more is better but good content comes at a cost. Plan whatever strategy best suits your business and budget, but don't just create it and leave it. Promote, analyse, improve and cut the waste when it makes sense.

Hyperlinks

Search engine crawlers explore the internet via links and the more interlinked the web is, the more they can find. In fact, without links, there would be no internet.

And it makes sense that these links have always been a way for search engines to determine what content is popular, who the authoritative sources are, and which content deserves a high rank. But the way in which links were originally used for ranking was too basic and too easily manipulated. You could just overuse keywords on a page, fire in as many links as possible with exact match anchor text... and boom! Number one!

It's not that easy nowadays. Google's Penguin update changed everything and today you have to be a lot smarter and more careful. In many ways, you just have to be more genuine.

Why links matter

Links still matter and are still one of the most important ranking factors, but today members of the SEO community find themselves needing to act more like marketers and less like spammers. Unfortunately, there are still a lot of people out there offering services that would have been more effective in the 'noughties' but still labelling them as 'white hat'.

Assuming that you care about your business, let's ignore those 'I can guarantee you #1 position in Google' emails and crack on with some real work.

It's worth talking a little about Google guidelines before we continue here, because some of us are ultra-cautious and some not-so-cautious. Put simply, Google doesn't like links that were placed solely for the purpose of influencing rankings. Some people seem to take that as meaning Google won't allow you to do anything: outreach of any kind, guest posting, asking to be added to a popular resource page. But people need to be a bit more relaxed about it. This is marketing, after all. If you've created great content, why wouldn't you promote it? Why wouldn't you ask a high-traffic site to share or link to it and drive referral traffic? Why wouldn't you put a guest post on a really popular site where your target audience spends time, and then mention something of value on your site or just your brand in general? And not everything has to be about ranking. In fact, focusing only on that is more likely to have you wandering down a pointless path. There's no value in creating Web 2.0 sites that no one will ever see, or asking for link placements on sites that don't receive any traffic. If Google doesn't value the site enough to rank it, why would it value a link from there?

By all means think like a marketer; don't lock yourself in a bunker and never do anything for fear of getting slapped on the wrists by Google because you've got a popular guest post with a branded link in it that you had the cheek to ask for.

Outreach and link building

Let's start with a truth bomb: getting links is hard. Admittedly, this can often depend on the size of the brand and the company's budgets, but for most sites it's not easy. A huge brand with huge budgets can gain massive traction online (for example, if you sell little plastic building blocks, you could make a movie about them. Genius!) Most businesses don't have the budgets to go and make a Hollywood blockbuster, though, so we have to make the most of what we do have.

Let's look at some popular, affordable options. We've already looked at a few ways of earning and encouraging links in the Content section – things like ego bait and expert roundups. Those people may well link to those pieces of content. Their followers may well link to them too.

Sitting back and hoping for the best is a surefire way to hear nothing but crickets, and that's where outreach comes in. Have people linked to or shared similar content before? Let them know about it. Would influencers in your industry like your content? Let them know about it. Are there popular bloggers on similar topics in your industry who would love to share your content? Let them know about it. It's all about promotion, about marketing. Shout about your cracking content.

Let's look at a few other methods.

Competitor links

Looking at your competitors is often a good place to start. Who links to the market leaders? Are there sites that link to multiple competitors but not to you? Why aren't they linking to you? How can you change that? You may already have checked what content is performing well for your competitors; who links to that? Are they reaching audiences you're not? Examining your competitors' content links could give you huge insights into the people and sites you should be talking to and which audiences you're missing out on. The next step is to do something about it.

Broken link building

Whether you frown upon asking for a link or not, surely no one can frown upon being helpful? There are many ways to do broken link building. One method is to find long-form content that links out a lot, or high-quality resource pages relevant to your business or content, and then run a link check. Chrome extensions like 'Check My Links' do a great job of this. You can run it on the pages you've found and check them for broken links. Approaching a site owner by helpfully highlighting this issue on their page is a great way to open a conversation. They may even like to consider replacing that broken link with a similar, maybe even better resource. You know what I'm saying.

The skyscraper technique

I've mentioned the skyscraper technique already, but it deserves a quick mention here too because it's not only about great content but also the links and shares it can bring. Once you have content that's ten times better than anything else on the web, it's time to promote it. As well as considering general outreach to industry relevant sites, blogs and influencers, it's also time to look at similar content that performed well previously. Who linked to that? If they liked that content, they're bound to like something that's ten times better. Who shared it? If they liked it enough to share it, they'll probably love yours... You get the idea.

Guest posting

This is perhaps a controversial one, and it's one that still confuses people. Opinions may differ but I'm a fan of guest posting. A lot of people panicked when ex-Googler Matt Cutts said 'Stick A Fork In It, Guest Blogging Is Done'.[4] But he did also say, 'I did a follow-up video to warn folks away from *spammy guest articles*'. Guest posting took a hit, but it wasn't the sort of guest posting I'm talking about here. At the time of Matt's 'fork' quote there was a popular guest blogging network which worked wonders for ranking sites. The general idea of this network was that you'd write a post, place a strategic link, upload it to the site and then someone else in the network would pick it up and place it on their site. Boom! Easy link! The trouble was that it was just that. A crappy link on a crappy site, put there purely for SEO purposes. When Google picked up on the existence of networks like this, it hit them hard.

But let's step back from the dark side for a moment. What about the good side of guest posting? Some really good online publications, blogs, whatever you want to call them, have been built around guest posts. And why not? It's pretty much how many newspapers and magazines work, and you wouldn't hit them for being spammy.

---

4   M. Cutts, 'Gadgets, Google, and SEO: The decay and fall of guest blogging for SEO' (Google/SEO, 2014) https://mattcutts.com/blog /guest-blogging

So step out, close the bunker door behind you, and stop worrying about something that's genuine marketing, brand exposure, publicity and a potential means of referring traffic. Sure, it might also help with rankings if the sites are relevant and high-quality – but that's just an added bonus. A great one.

Before you run off and create hundreds of 500-word posts and hammer them out to anyone who will take them, though, consider a few things:

- Is this a genuine site/business?

- Does this site get traffic? (I'll say it again: if Google doesn't value the site, why should they value a link from it?)

- Is the content you're submitting great content?

- Is it relevant to the site? (Should you really be guest posting about scuba diving on someone's dog training blog?)

Anchor text

I can hear some of you saying, 'But if I'm not asking for links, surely I won't have control over the anchor text?' It's like this: whether you're white hat, grey hat or you don't even like hats, at some point you're probably going to have control of some anchor text. So, you should understand why it's more important than ever and why you need to be aware of it.

It used to be common practice to use exact match anchors for almost every link you could get pointing to a page. Even if these were site-wide such as footer or sidebar links, then that was still great; the more the better. Even putting keyword anchors into the home-page was common practice.

Things are close to the opposite of that now.

Look at the backlink profiles of some well-established leading brands and you'll see a common theme: highly branded profiles, with almost all of the homepages being some sort of brand or URL variation:

Brand

brand.com

www.brand.com

https://www.brand.com

There may be some natural anchors like 'click here' and maybe the occasional keyword, but if a homepage had a lot of links, you'd expect most of them to be branded.

When you look at these brands' deeper pages, you'll see a good, natural-looking mix of anchors; it will rarely be a long list of keywords. Of course, there will almost certainly be keywords in there, but think about it realistically. If site owners link to a site, would they all use the same anchor text? It's unlikely. And that is what you'll notice with these brands: occasional keyword, some variations, partial matches, longer anchors that mention the keyword or part of the keyword, synonyms, LSI, natural anchors like 'this product' and also some more branded and URL anchors.

All of this means that if you have a page that you're hoping will acquire some well-deserved links, it's worth being aware of its current anchor text distribution. Using Ahrefs or Majestic, or combining data from both, is a good way to get this information. You can then compare it with the rest of page 1 for your target's terms or topics – or even just with the top five. They can act as a good benchmark, but use their data with a pinch of salt. If a couple of sites use more exact match anchors than you were expecting to see, it's always possible that they've disavowed these and asked Google to ignore them.

TOP TIP

When checking the anchor text distribution for your whole site, you would expect to see it heavily branded and mostly to the homepage.

When analysing pages, look out for overuse of exact match anchors.

If you have any control over anchors, don't immediately opt for exact match. What does your current distribution for that page look like? Will the proposed anchor make sense to the user?

There are plenty of other options like variations, long tail, synonyms, URLs and so on.

Private blog networks

People still have huge networks of independent sites that have been built to look like genuine blogs or businesses. They are often built on expired domains or auction domains with good existing backlink profiles and therefore they have some good authority. Links from these sites can then help the target site or sites. That's the theory, but this is not going to be an instructional guide on setting up a private blog network (PBN) and I certainly won't be telling you the best way to do it to fool Google.

One or two public figures within the industry have said that PBNs don't work anymore, but that's simply not true. Many PBNs have been hit hard but some of the better ones still work extremely well. Does that mean I'd recommend it as a tactic? Absolutely not. Even people who have made fortunes thanks to PBNs are starting to go completely white hat. But why stop if this technique still has the potential to work well? Because it won't work forever. If you care about your business, then using risky tactics is a sure way to get hit further down the line.

The subject of backlinks is always a highly debatable one. People will always disagree on certain aspects of link building but most of them will agree on one thing: links are important, and that's why they're a key part of the ANCHOR model.

Ongoing tasks

We've carried out a thorough audit, we've taken the next steps and implemented those recommendations and fixes, we've looked at our content assets (current and future) and we've planned our link building strategy. Now what?

That question is a bit like 'how long is a piece of string?' There is an endless amount to be creating, fixing and improving, all on an ongoing basis. Some people may do the bare minimum – but those aren't necessarily the people who win at SEO. It's important to remember that SEO is no longer a game of content, links, title tags and not much else. As Google starts to consider site quality, user experience, intent and relevance, so must those who deal with the SEO side of things for any website. It's true that areas like UX and conversion rate optimisation used to be someone else's job, and you'll still come across people with that opinion who think that these areas should be completely separate to SEO. It simply isn't the case. If organic traffic and rankings are suffering because of a UX issue, then that's absolutely SEO-related.

When Google introduced RankBrain in 2015, they said it was their third most important ranking factor.[5] The company has been clear about it being a machine learning system that helps with the processing of search results – but beyond that, they are careful about how much information they reveal. They certainly don't want people figuring out the ins and outs of how it works.

User metrics, user behaviour and click data are more important than a lot of people realise. We know a little about the effects that changes in these metrics can have from testing and observations throughout the community. That's one of the things I love about the digital marketing community: people are so open to sharing info and findings that may help others. There are examples of people experimenting with a tweet and asking for clicks to a page from a large number of people as a test, then seeing the page rankings jump. We've seen people optimise title tags and meta descriptions to improve their click-through rates in the search results, followed by ranking improvements. And even if you already have great content on page 1 of Google,

---

5   D. Sullivan, 'Meet RankBrain: The Artificial Intelligence That's Now Processing Google Search Results' (SearchEngineLand, 2015) https://searchengineland.com/meet-rankbrain-google-search-results-234386

that's not to say it can't be expanded to cover more of that topic.

It's also worth noting that Google's scoring of page content isn't necessarily done at a page level. I see plenty of very thin hub pages ranking for extremely competitive terms. In cases like that, it's likely that Google is looking at the supporting content and the way the topic is covered as a whole. That last part is really important. If you want to rank for a competitive topic, are you covering that topic thoroughly?

From click data to on-page tweaks, what can you be doing on an ongoing basis to help drive more organic traffic and revenue to your website? The list could go on and on, so I've tried to group some things together and list a few examples to inspire your planning.

Keyword research

In the Audit section, I spoke about doing general keyword research for a site. During the Ongoing phase, you're more likely to be looking at page and topic level keyword research – rather than looking at the site as a whole, you look at a specific topic and build your research around that. Who are the competitors specific to that page/topic? What areas should be covered within that topic? What variations and LSI terms are related to that topic? Everything should become specific to just that topic, so you can go into some real detail rather than generalising.

Content creation

We've covered content already and it should be obvious by now that this is an important part of your ongoing work. And whether the initial focus is on new or existing content very much depends on things like time, budget and current performance.

Content improvements and culls

This is a big one, but it's often neglected. How often do you see content that's been created with good intentions but then left to rot for years? I can almost guarantee that you have some on your own site and it may well be time for a content cull. That doesn't mean all your old content needs to go – although sometimes that is for the best – but there may be opportunities for improvement. Also, it doesn't just need to be the really old content that gets improved. If you're really on the ball with your content, you should be keeping an eye on how it's performing in the early stages.

There are plenty of ways to improve content. You can ask questions such as:

- Does my page/site completely cover the topic I'm trying to rank for?

- What are the top-ranking competitors for that topic doing?

- What data do I have access to that will help me improve this page?

TOP TIP

We have access to useful keyword data that can help with content improvements. Paid tools like SEMrush and Ahrefs – and even free tools like Google Search Console – give us access to huge amounts of keyword data that we can use. For example: for our target page, what are the 'low-hanging fruit' terms (usually around low page 1 and page 2 of Google)? Are we covering these elements of the topic well enough? Can we expand on our content and improve it to include them? Can we mix up our internal linking anchors to include some of the variations and make it clear to search engines and users that they are relevant to the topic?

On-page improvements

An obvious one, but worth a mention. Things like title tags are still important elements in terms of both keywords and relevance, as well as in attracting click-throughs. Are your on-page elements well-optimised? Are you using all the data available to you to tweak them? Just be sure to not over-optimise.

Internal linking improvements

We've discussed the importance of internal linking and you may already have looked at this aspect as part of the Next Steps phase. But as with most things SEO-related, this isn't a 'set it and forget it' job. Internal linking can be tested and improved on an ongoing basis.

TOP TIP

Link from old (relevant) posts to new content you've just posted.

Technical crawls and fixes

When you're dealing with a little ten-page WordPress site, you won't usually find many technical issues cropping up. When you have an ecommerce site with thousands of products, there's a lot more to go wrong. Depending on how you're dealing with out of stock items, discontinued items, and other changes to your categories and products, there are a number of issues that can occur over time: broken links, internal links going through redirects, incorrect sitemaps, orphaned pages and so on. Not keeping on top of these issues could have a negative impact on the perceived quality of your site so it's a good idea to run a fairly regular crawl to identify technical issues. The frequency of this check depends on your site and the regularity of change and likely issues, but a monthly crawl would be a good starting point.

Conversion rate optimisation (split) testing

Your traffic is looking good, but you really wish that conversion rate would improve. Often, people will address this by just working on getting more traffic. Sound familiar? But if more revenue is the ultimate goal, why not also work on improving the conversion rate? It's a no-brainer, right? Tools like Optimizely make it easy for non-coders to make simple HTML changes to a page and split test them against the live page. If the results are positive, you can bring in the developers to make the change permanent. The value of split testing often depends on your levels of traffic – but if you currently have enough traffic to produce conclusive results, you really must try it. I've seen significant improvements in conversions and revenue from the simplest of split tests that provided conclusive and sometimes surprising insights.

Outreach and link building

Link building is by no means a job you only do once; being consistent with it is important for keeping growth alive. It's like the blood pumping through your veins – and turning it off probably won't do you any favours. I was once asked to look at the performance of a clothing ecommerce site. It was a fairly well-established brand, but they said they hadn't done much online marketing for a while. Using tools to look at their online visibility, I could see a clear and steady decline over the preceding two years, but only now had they realised they needed to do something about it. Imagine where they could have been if they hadn't had that long period of inactivity. Stopping SEO activity doesn't halt traffic in the way that stopping paid campaigns does, but it will cause traffic to decline over time.

Although we have already discussed link building, here are a few other examples to get the ideas flowing:

- Interviews and comments – responding to journalist requests

- Being featured in product guides

- Giveaways and competitions

This isn't an extensive guide to link building but hopefully you have enough food for thought to realise there are plenty of ways to increase the number of quality links to your website.

However you decide to market your business, consistency is important. Put a plan in place, create processes, create schedules and do the work.

Review

The Review element is not just about reporting; it's also about finding areas for improvement, low-hanging fruit and stuff you can action during the next phase of ongoing tasks. There are countless tools out there to help but we're going to concentrate on Google Analytics and Google Search Console, because they're the main ones, and they're free.

Google Analytics

I'm sure most of you check your analytics fairly regularly, or at least get analytics reports from your team. But I know there will be some of you who never check any of this stuff, and even the odd few who don't have any analytics installed. Before I continue, then: if you don't check your analytics or have someone checking it for you on a regular basis – start now. You need to know where your traffic is coming from, how well your different channels are converting, which categories and products are performing, what performs best seasonally, and so on.

Most of those who do check it will just be looking at traffic, revenue and conversion data. This is OK for a top-level overview but there's so much more you could be doing. Most analytics tools have powerful features and filters and although I will be talking mostly about Google Analytics, most of what I cover will also be relevant to other platforms.

Google Search Console

As well as Google Analytics, we should talk a little about Google Search Console (formerly Webmaster Tools) because it's another key part of the review process. I still come across plenty of sites that don't have Search Console installed. If this is you, get it set up today. There are so many benefits to having it; it's also required for submitting sitemaps to Google and doing a disavow if needed. I heard a web agency saying, 'We didn't set up Search Console as we didn't see the need for it.' *Every* site should have Google Search Console set up.

Let's look at just a few of the features and benefits of Search Console:

Keyword data

Search Console is the only Google tool that still gives you access to keyword data for your site. Is it 100%

accurate? The jury's very much out on that one but whether it's accurate or not, there's a goldmine of data sitting here – and it's free.

Performance

Even if some people are sceptical about the accuracy of the data, Search Console gives you a great way to track your performance trends over time. It's also broken down further, allowing you to track impressions (how often you're appearing in search), click-through rate (CTR) and average rankings, as well as clicks. This is not only great for tracking performance trends, it's also useful for finding CTR issues at the page or query level. For example: what queries are you ranking well for, getting high impressions but a terrible CTR? Having identified these, you can then look at the relevance of that term to the page and what the title tag and meta description are saying. Do these match intent? How can you improve them? You can do so much with the Performance section of Search Console. It can be the driving force behind content improvements, as well as a diagnostics tool for times when there are traffic declines.

Indexing status and crawl issues

If you go to Google and type 'site: *your domain with TLD*' you'll see how many of your pages Google has indexed. There may be a thousand, there may be hundreds of thousands. Either way, this is just a long list of search results, and it's not much use when you want to know what *hasn't* been indexed, or what's been indexed but shouldn't have been. The Coverage section of Search Console digs into a number of aspects of your indexing status: pages that were blocked by robots.txt but have been indexed, URLs with server errors, pages that are set to noindex but are in your XML sitemap, and so on.

Submitting and checking XML sitemaps

The Coverage area also allows you to submit your website's XML sitemap (so that Google can find and read it) and look for errors and warnings within it, which are then highlighted by Search Console.

Uploading disavow files

The disavow tool is still useful for getting Google to ignore terrible backlinks. When they launched version

4.0 of their Penguin update, the general understanding was that Google would just ignore bad links. Yet I've still seen examples of the disavow file seemingly doing its job towards helping a struggling site. And, worryingly, I still hear of examples of negative SEO working. (Negative SEO is basically the process of hammering someone else's website with spammy links that are completely against Google's guidelines, to drop them in the rankings. It's totally unethical and an awful path to go down.)

Poor links can also have an impact on the anchor text distribution. If I think the current backlink profile of a site is really poor and could potentially hold the site back, I'm still more than happy to use the disavow file. Some people don't bother with it these days, but I say don't discount it just yet.

Finding malware issues

This is another useful feature of Search Console and hopefully it's one you'll never need. But if your site were to be hit with malware issues and you didn't have Search Console, would you have a clue how to diagnose it?

Manual penalty notifications

Another feature that I hope you'll never have to use –
but if someone has done some terrible link building
for you in the past, or you've been hit by negative
SEO, Search Console is the only place you can pick up
a notification of a manual penalty from Google. You
can then do something about it.

For this and many other reasons, why wouldn't you
always have Search Console set up for your website?
Do it now.

Digging into the data

Examples of use cases for Google Analytics could make
a book in their own right, and it would be much bigger
than this one. But let's look at some key uses and tips
to make sure you're getting the most from the ocean
of data in front of you.

Key metrics

When you're reviewing your data on Google Analytics
and Google Search Console, first decide what metrics

you're going to monitor on a regular basis. What's important to you may depend on the nature of your business, but there will be certain metrics that are more meaningful for you than others. Often these are fairly standard. For example, in Google Analytics, you can monitor and report on sessions, users, users per session, bounce rate (only on certain pages), revenue, ecommerce conversion rate, top performing categories and products and so on.

It will sound obvious to most, but do also make sure you have ecommerce tracking set up so that you can track your transaction and revenue data.

Digging deeper

Segmentation, segmentation, segmentation. Analytics can split your data by device, medium, product types, areas of your website, and it's often important to narrow your data like this to cut out the noise. Has traffic climbed but revenue stayed flat? Perhaps mobile users have been responsible for the traffic increase – these users generally have lower conversion rates as they're often just researching products on mobile devices before making the purchase on desktop. That climb in traffic is great, but it could be misleading in terms of revenue-driving traffic. Having this kind of insight could enable you to improve that mobile experience. Is the product the type of purchase the user would normally discuss with their other half? Are they able to share the product details quickly and easily?

There are endless examples of why segmenting the data is important so before jumping to conclusions when you're looking at the key metrics, dig a little deeper.

You should also be digging into data around landing pages. Work out where your traffic is coming in. Also look at exit pages; where are you losing users? Are they dead ends?

Funnels

Funnels can be used to track the path your users take on their way to a sale. Often made up of particular goal pages, a funnel can allow you to see how many people are following the desired route, and the drop-off rates. Think about set pages that you want people to go through when completing a form submission or a product purchase (basket, checkout etc). Yes, you want more traffic to your site – but you can also see big gains in revenue just from improving your conversion rate. Do you have a leaky funnel?

Low-hanging fruit

Low-hanging fruit can be an important thing to consider in the review process if you're looking for opportunities. There are many ways to look at low-hanging fruit, from extremely simple angles to more in-depth analysis and opportunity finding. Both Google Analytics and Google Search Console – as well as a host of other tools such as Ahrefs and SEMrush – are great for this kind of work.

First of all: what is 'low-hanging fruit'? Depending on who you talk to, you'll hear different definitions and different ways of doing things. Put simply, low-hanging fruit refers to the quick wins and opportunities that you're almost there with but that just need a little bump. For example, when you hit the top three positions in Google, you'll often see a big difference in traffic. And obviously, jumping from page 2 to page 1 of Google will also make a difference. (Where's the best place to hide a dead body? Page 2 of Google. Sorry – awful, I know, but not my joke.) Focusing on improving your terms that are ranking in positions 4–20, for example, can quickly result in more traffic and conversions.

These opportunities could be found from individual terms you're tracking, from the average ranking data of a page in Search Console, or from ranking data in those other third-party tools.

TOP TIP

If you have limited budgets for new content, go for the low-hanging fruit.

A few other things to think about

- Are your numbers right? Check that Google Analytics is implemented correctly according to best practice. Common issues are the code not being on the correct part of the page and the old code being left on the page when switching over to Google Tag Manager. If you have a zero bounce rate, this is normally because the code is being triggered twice; you get a double fire, which means 0% bounce.

- Are all of your referrals genuine referrals? Check self-referrals from payment gateways.

- Get your foundations right. Make sure your Google Analytics views are set up correctly, eg Master (unfiltered), Live and Test (copy of Live).

- Keep it tidy. Ensure that you're using UTM ('Urchin tracking module') tracking codes correctly. Common errors include putting source and medium the wrong way round, or using different case (Analytics will keep them separate). If you're running a campaign across a number of mediums, give them all the same campaign name so that you can look at the campaign as a whole and then split it by source and medium to see how each part is performing.

- Think outside the box. Add some custom dimensions for custom tracking of things that are unique to your site.

PART THREE

What Else?

Someone asked me a while back, 'What are the three key things you should have to drive successful growth to an ecommerce business?'

It was a fairly easy one to answer but I loved the way it was put and the way it made me think. There are so many elements to marketing, but I summed it up as:

- SEO

- Paid strategies

- List building and email marketing

Into the blender

Throwing all those things in a blender together can work wonders. I've seen multiple businesses built from the ground up with SEO as their main focus and driver; I've seen a seven-figure business built from nothing with a huge focus on pay-per-click (PPC), although that was back when things were a little cheaper; and I've seen a large media business with a huge portfolio of leading sites make a huge chunk of its revenue via email marketing. Those are just a few examples of these three amazing strategies. Combining them gives you a focus on three of the strongest acquisition channels, rather than just one, and it can often be a reliable mix that grows and grows over time.

SEO is a long-term strategy, but an important one. Paid can be a quicker win – but if you turn it off it can be bye-bye, traffic and revenue. Email is a great channel, but you have to play it well and you can't be constantly visible. Put them all together, though, and... Kapow! Any weaknesses become less significant because the channels support each other so well.

In this section, we'll look at these other two channels, as well as taking a look at the how and who of getting everything done.

Paid strategies for ecommerce

'Paid strategies' sounds like a pretty broad term, right? There are multiple paid strategies that work well for ecommerce and I'm going to talk about what I think are the strongest of those: Google Ads, Google Shopping, Facebook ads, Instagram ads and Amazon Ads.

It's hard to dispute the massive potential Google offers ecommerce businesses. There are around 75,000 Google searches per second and counting.[1] And although there have been significant algorithmic and search layout changes since 2014, on average 50.1% of all website traffic still comes from organic search.[2]

Ranking well in the search engines can take time, however, and it's often the result of a consistent, focused strategy that includes multiple on-site and off-site tactics such as those in the ANCHOR model. Incorporating some shorter-term tactics into your traffic strategy can help you move the needle faster.

---

1   Internet Live Stats https://internetlivestats.com/one-second/
    #google-band
2   BrightEdge, 'Organic Search Is Still the Largest Channel' (2017
    report) https://brightedge.com/resources/research-reports/content
    -optimization

Short-term strategies can help you to validate and test new products, raise brand awareness and rapidly drive targeted traffic to your ecommerce website. It's important to diversify your traffic sources to make sure you stay competitive and remain afloat should one channel fail.

Here are some complementary channels to support your SEO efforts so you can generate some consistent, targeted traffic to your ecommerce business.

Google Ads

If you want to compete with larger brands and show up in Google's search results for your target key-words, investing in Google Ads has become almost unavoidable.

Years ago, organic results graced the top of Google's pages. But Google now pushes them down to the bottom of the fold (and sometimes below it) and puts paid ads in their place. And since about 50% of internet users can no longer tell the difference between Google Ads and organic search results, it's now necessary to invest in Google Ads if you want to rank in those coveted 'above the fold' spots.[3]

Google Ads costs

Investing money into Google Ads can be problematic for ecommerce marketers as Google Ad prices (cost per click, CPC) in general continue to rise.

However, research has shown that in 2017 and 2018 there were wide fluctuations in CPC for Google search ads.[4]/[5] While it rose more than 200% from Q1 2017 to Q1 2018, prices dropped more than 200% in 2018. So while a five- to seven-year analysis might show prices increasing, CPC for Google Ads fluctuates monthly and yearly depending on the market.

Even with costs rising, Google Ads is still a powerful media play for ecommerce stores. While SEO is a

3   E. Gabbert, '5 Reasons to Diversify Your Search Strategy with PPC Advertising' (WordStream, 2015) https://wordstream.com/blog/ws /2012/07/18/diversify-search-strategy-ppc

4   J. D. Prater, *Q4 2017 Paid Search and Paid Social Benchmark Report* (AdStage, 2017) https://cdn2.hubspot.net/hubfs/4350015 /Benchmark%20Report/AdStage%20Q4%20%20PPC%20Benchmark %20Report.pdf

5   AdStage, *Q4 2018 Benchmark Report* (2018) https://cdn2.hubspot .net/hubfs/4350015/Q4%202018%20Paid%20Media%20Benchmark %20Report%20(2).pdf

long-term play, Google Ads allows you to 'cheat' the organic rankings and get on key search engine pages quickly. Bear in mind that ecommerce retailers enjoy the highest click-through rates of all industries (5.23%) for Google search PPC ads.[6]

Your CPC is also directly tied to your target keyword, market competition and quality score, all of which you have control over. With a few tweaks, you can raise your quality score and lower your CPC.

Qualified traffic and remarketing

The traffic Google Ads brings is qualified, which means it will be targeted to your visitors' interests. By bidding on specific targeted keywords, you can create ads that direct consumers to the most relevant landing page. This will enable you to continue the conversation from user search query to landing page, increasing the chance of a conversion.

---

6   C. Soames, 'Google Ads conversion rate averages by industry' (SmartInsights, 2018) https://smartinsights.com/paid-search -marketing-ppc/paid-search-display-network/google-adwords -conversion-rate-averages-by-industry-infographic

Did the user visit a product page and then abandon your store? With Google Ads, you can remarket to those people and get your products in front of them again, serving them ads based on their unique interests and behaviours. Remarketing is a powerful strategy because it targets potential customers who are already aware of your brand.

Google Shopping

Formerly called Product Listing Ads, Google Shopping ads have been around since 2010; although they are a newer addition to the Google Ad stack, they have picked up speed quickly. They have even overtaken Google text ads in retail search ad spend at 76.4% in the US and 82% in the UK. Google Shopping ads also attract 85.3% and 87.9% of paid search clicks in the US and UK respectively.[7]

Google Shopping ads are powerful because they match user intent with search results. Users are shown ads based on products they are already interested in buying and this increases conversion rates. This strategy

---

7   Adthena, 'The Rise of Google Shopping', *Adthena Search Advertising Report* (2018) https://cdn2.hubspot.net/hubfs/546369/Gated %20Content%20PDFs/Adthena-Google-Shopping-Report-2018.pdf

removes some of the consumer's shopping journey friction, giving users the ability to shop for their desired products directly from Google search results and then click to buy easily.

Preferable to Google text ads in search

Data also suggests that for ecommerce businesses, Google Shopping ads may be superior to Google text ads.

Google Shopping ads enable you to showcase and sell your products directly in the search results. The ads include product images, descriptions, prices and reviews, displayed in a carousel format. This is superior to Google text ads in that searchers can see immediately what your product looks like; this can attract more clicks than simple text.

In addition, your product ads can appear more than once for each user query, giving you more opportunities to attract customers. They can also appear in image search results.

Continuous improvements

Google also continues to improve the look of its shopping ads and often experiments with new layouts.

Product ads sat below text ads until 2015, when they were relocated to the top of the search results page. In 2016, Google removed text ads from the side rail, making the Google Shopping product ads more prominent. Current searches reveal product categories, which now sit atop the product images where appropriate, giving users the opportunity to search either by price or by product attribute. Google also pulls special offers (eg free shipping) from your feed and showcases them within the ad block.

Facebook and Instagram ads

By the end of 2018, Facebook had over 2.3 billion users, making it a viable channel for ecommerce businesses trying to get more brand and product exposure. Though Facebook ad revenue sits second to Google, the platform is still widely popular among marketers with a return on investment (ROI) averaging 152%.[8]

Instagram, though it is a newer platform than Facebook and has fewer users (1 billion as of June 2018), is slowly becoming the preferred channel among marketers.

---

8   J. Slegg, *Facebook Retail Advertisers Averaging 152% ROI Report* (Search Engine Watch, 2013) https://searchenginewatch.com/sew/study /2301423/facebook-retail-advertisers-averaging-152-roi-report

Instagram users tend to be more engaged than Facebook users, resulting in rapid growth for advertisers.

Costs and targeting

On the whole, marketers like Facebook and Instagram ads because they cost less than Google. The average CPCs for Google Ads (search) and Facebook are $2.69 and $1.72 respectively.[9]/[10]

Besides the low cost of running Facebook ads, you can get more granular with your targeting – you can target particular consumer interests and behaviours – and even cast a wider net to reach more people by targeting 'lookalike' audiences.

Although Facebook and Instagram advertising can yield high returns, the success of your ads will depend less on stats and more on your targeting and ad creative. If your audience doesn't respond to your ads, your

---

9   M. Irvine, 'Google Ads Benchmarks for YOUR Industry [Updated!]: Paid Search Marketing', *The WordStream Blog* (WordStream, 2019) https://wordstream.com/blog/ws/2016/02/29/google-adwords -industry-benchmarks

10 M. Irvine, 'Google Ads Benchmarks for YOUR Industry [Updated!]: Social Media', *The WordStream Blog* (WordStream, 2019) https:// wordstream.com/blog/ws/2017/02/28/facebook-advertising -benchmarks

CPC will be high (and your ROI low) regardless of the platform you are using.

Differences with Google Ads (social vs. search)

One other thing to note is that, in contrast to Google users, Facebook and Instagram users are not primarily using the platforms to shop; your ads will be more intrusive to them. Users visit Google with a specific intent to find the answer to their query, and hopefully with an intent to buy something. Facebook and Instagram users visit those platforms to connect and share. Anything that interrupts that activity may be construed as a distraction.

For that reason, focus your social ad campaigns first on brand awareness and lead generation (if applicable) instead of quick sales. Your audience will likely not be as far along in the buying cycle as those searching on Google. Be helpful and give value. Once you gain some website visitors, focus your ad campaigns on retargeting your visitors based on their past behaviours (visited your product page, abandoned the cart etc) to get them back to your store to finish their purchase.

Amazon Ads

Amazon Ads have only been around since 2012, but they have quickly become a formidable advertising channel for ecommerce. Though Amazon's ad revenue pales against that of Facebook and Google, it still snagged 4.1% of total US digital ad spending in 2018.[11] This percentage is predicted to continue growing in the years to come. As of Q3 2018, Amazon showed a 123% increase in ad sales, hitting $2.5 billion for the quarter with 29% year on year revenue growth.[12]

Is Amazon a good channel for ecommerce businesses? For one, they are the largest e-retailer in the US. In a recent study, 71% of participants who advertised on Amazon reported that they spent up to a quarter of their digital ad budget on the platform, and 80% of participants planned to increase Amazon advertising budgets, with nearly a quarter of them increasing budgets by 50% or more.[13]

---

11   M. Dolliver, 'Some Bad (and Good) News for Facebook in 2019' (Marketer, 2019) https://emarketer.com/content/predicting-some -bad-news-and-good-news-for-facebook-in-2019

12   A. Gesenhues, 'Amazon reports 3rd straight quarter of triple-digit ad revenue growth' (Martech: Management, 2018) https:// martechtoday.com/amazon-reports-3rd-straight-quarter-of-triple -digit-ad-revenue-growth-227047

13   C. Dobson, 'Study: 71% of Amazon Advertisers Spend 25% of Digital Ad Budgets on Amazon' (LSA Insider, 2018) https://lsainsider.com /study-71-of-amazon-advertisers-spend-25-of-digital-ad-budgets-on -amazon/archives

High purchase intent

One of the biggest advantages of using Amazon Ads is the goal of users navigating the website. Users searching Amazon are there to buy – their purchase intent is high. By targeting users in buying mode, the ads are much more likely to convert. In fact, the average conversion rate for advertisers on Amazon is 9.78%, compared with typical ecommerce conversion rates of 1.33%.[14] Similar to Google Ads, Amazon also offers a display ad network (Amazon DSP) that allows you to show your ads on Amazon-owned online properties such as IMDb.

Bringing it all together

What you can do with paid channels often depends on your budgets, but if you have the funds to try these channels then you should at least be testing them. If you can get a good return, then why wouldn't you use all these channels? If you can combine a solid SEO strategy with good ad returns, you're on your way to becoming a force to be reckoned with…

---

14 The Badger, 'Amazon Advertising Stats: 2019 Update' (AdBadger, 2019) https://adbadger.com/blog/amazon-advertising-stats

But what's missing?

How about 'the list'? Do you have a database of customers and potential customers? Are you making the most of that data? Let's look at email marketing and the ways in which it can complement the other channels.

Email marketing: the money's in the list

Email marketing is a low-cost channel to get your brand in front of more consumers and to entice current customers to repurchase. Unlike advertising, email marketing allows you to build relationships with your customers, encouraging trust and long-term loyalty – the backbone of customer retention. By running a successful email campaign, you can build an army of loyal subscribers who will then trust you enough to buy your products when you promote them. Email marketing enjoys a 4,400% ROI in the US – that is, marketers can earn $44 for every $1 they spend on campaigns[15] – and the ROI in the UK is $38 for every $1 spent (based on one study; statistics from other studies

---

15   Campaign Monitor, 'Year in Review', *Annual Report* (2016) https://campaignmonitor.com/company/annual-report/2016

may differ).[16] This form of marketing can also drive consistent automated revenue and increase customer retention. You can automate cart, category and checkout abandonment sequences, personalise welcome messages based on customer preferences, and offer product recommendations – all via email.

The key with email marketing is to always add value and to focus on personalising messages based on subscriber preferences and behaviour (eg purchase history and browsing activity). The more a subscriber feels valued, the more likely they will remain a subscriber and take advantage of your offers.

Value is an important word when it comes to email marketing but people often seem to miss that. How many times have you unsubscribed from an email list because it was all 'sales, sales, sales' and nothing else? Admittedly, if the emails come from a business whose discounts you're always on the lookout for, you may check them regularly. If not, you're more likely to feel pestered – unless there's additional value there. If you want the people on your list to be long-term customers, build long-term relationships.

---

16   *DMA National Client Email Report* (emailmonday, 2015) https://emailmonday.com/dma-national-client-email-report-2015

Automation

There are loads of elements to a great email marketing strategy but since it's not the focus of this book, I'm not going to delve into all of them. However, automation is a key element for ecommerce email marketing and whether email is a focus for you or not, you should have at least some of the following set up:

- **Welcome email/series.** Real-time welcome emails tend to get great open rates. A popular way to get users to sign up is by offering an incentive, such as a discount on the first order. And why not build on that with a well-planned series of follow-up emails?

- **Abandoned cart emails.** Has someone added something to the basket and then left the site? Assuming you have their email address, an abandoned cart email can often deliver a great return on what may otherwise be a lost sale.

- **Up-sells and cross-sells.** After a sale, there's a great opportunity to convince the customer to buy a related item or something that would complement their purchase. Did they just buy a suit? How about showing them the top picks of shoes and ties?

- **Re-engagement.** This is an important one, especially if your products have a repeat buying cycle. For example, if you sell protein powders, you might want to send an email to a customer three weeks after their purchase, reminding them to restock.

Other tips

There are a lot of pieces to the puzzle when it comes to getting email marketing right. Here are a few more tips for inspiration and to get you thinking about what you might be missing:

- **Segment your list.** If you can do this well and customise your emails for specific segments, your open rates and conversion rates will be much higher.

- **CTAs.** Include a clear call to action in your emails.

- **Don't be boring.** Whether it's a thank you email, an order confirmation or a promotion, catch the user's attention.

- **Test, test, test.** Test subject lines, landing pages etc. What works best? What can you improve?

- **Personalisation.** This can mean a number of things – from displaying the customer's name to showing them products relevant to their purchase history. Personalising emails can be a great way to grab attention and it can make a big difference to their performance.

- **Optimise your emails to get past spam filters.** If they end up in spam folders – or even the 'Promotions' tab in Gmail – they're much less likely ever to be opened.

- **Think mobile first.** More than half of your readers will likely be reading the email on their phone. Make sure it's optimised for mobile devices.

- **Use images.** This goes without saying, especially for ecommerce businesses.

- **Ask for reviews.** Not only can reviews act as testimonials that others can read, they can also give you valuable feedback about your products and service.

- **Reward loyalty.** Make sure loyalty is rewarded.

- **Referral schemes.** Consider having a referral scheme.

- **Track and measure.** Set up email campaign tracking so that you can measure performance in Google Analytics. You should also be tracking your open and click-through rates. How can you improve these?

- **Remember that email is two-way.** Please don't use a no-reply email address. You might as well say, 'Hey, listen to us but don't bother replying because we haven't got the time or the interest to take any notice.'

The list

What's the point in having email marketing if there's no one on your list? You're probably building up a list of customers, but you should also be building a 'hot list' of *potential* customers – and they should be the right ones. Would you rather have a list of 100,000 people who are never likely to buy from you, or 10,000 warm potential customers who are highly relevant? Having a *targeted* list is key. Here are some tactics that all ecommerce businesses can use to expand the size of their list:

- **Generic email opt-in forms.** For instance, the ones you see in the top bar of a page, in the footer or maybe in the sidebar of the blog.

- **Pop-ups and incentivised emails.** These are usually timed or exit intent pop-ups that offer a discount on the first online order.

- **Lead magnets.** Whether it's a downloadable guide, a template, a checklist or some free training material, make sure it's relevant to your target market, and that it's valuable and high-quality.

- **Content upgrades.** These are a form of lead magnet offered within content, and they are usually relevant to that content (eg a checklist related to a blog post).

- **Giveaways.** Make sure they are relevant. I've seen people running competitions to win an iPad, only to collect a huge amount of email addresses from people who have no interest whatsoever in their products. Make sure the prize is relevant only to your target market.

Who should do the work?

How do you go about getting the wheels in motion – and who do you get to do it all? It goes without saying that this is massively dependent on a number of factors: the size of your business, the size of your current team and resources, your marketing budgets, the time available, and so on. The most common options are doing it all yourself, using an in-house team, or outsourcing the work – usually to a freelancer, a team of freelancers, or an agency. All of these options come with their own pros and cons.

You

At this point, some of you may just be saying, 'Nope!' and turning to the next section. Let me make it clear now that no one should be doing all of this stuff alone. But at the same time, you need to have at least some role, even if it's just oversight and being aware of what's happening.

Depending on your position in the business, the amount you do will vary. For example, if you're an ecommerce business owner, you most likely won't want to do much, if any, of the work discussed so far. And rightly so – your job is to run your business, not to spend your days auditing your site, creating content or doing outreach. You should, however, at least be aware of what's going on and how things are performing, even if you have someone in your team managing everything else. If you're that person – perhaps the marketing manager or the ecommerce director – then of course you'll need to be aware of what's being done (by your team, the freelancers, the agency), the results of that work, and the planned improvements. You may even have an active role in one or more of the ANCHOR elements. And if you're one of those team members, you'll obviously be doing your specific job and should be aware of everything else that's happening from an online marketing point of view.

But whatever your role, you shouldn't be doing everything. That's just not realistic; you can't audit a site, then implement all the changes, create amazing content, then do all of the outreach, all of the ongoing improvements, all of the analysis and planning, on your own. And if you do, it will be a sub-par job.

If you're a business owner wanting to do it yourself to save money – stop. You're almost certainly not an expert writer, an outreach specialist, a technical SEO *and* a Google Analytics guru. Even if you are, I'm certain that if you're also running a business, you don't have time to do all of that as well. And if you're an in-house SEO or marketing executive tasked with doing 'the online marketing' for an entire ecommerce business, no matter what size, you shouldn't be doing everything yourself, either.

I regularly speak to people who say they run all of the online marketing for a business. No freelancers, no in-house support; just them. And if they're not smashing it out of the park and hitting all of their targets, they shouldn't be surprised, and neither should their employer. Finding a good jack-of-all-trades isn't easy and it certainly isn't cheap. If you are that person, you may well be struggling to get everything done. You might find that you lack skills in some of the areas you're responsible for. Be straight with your boss and tell them that having support in those areas would make the overall strategy much more effective. For example, you might be good at SEO in general but not a great writer. Good writing takes time and is a quite separate skill from online marketing; ask your boss for a content budget and find some good freelance writers.

Whatever your role in the business, you cannot do everything. It may be the cheap option, but the decision-makers in the business need to be realistic if they want their online strategy to succeed. If a rugby team wants to cut costs and only sends the fly-half onto the field, they might manage to land a few penalties here and there but they're certainly not going to win the match – and they're going to feel pretty battered and bruised afterwards. Get the point?

Pros

- Cheap

Cons

- One person can't do everything – they probably don't have all of the skills required, or the time

- More likely to end up in sub-par results

- The person is likely to become demoralised

In-house

Some large businesses have the 'luxury' of having a fully skilled in-house team at their disposal. This certainly has its advantages but can also come with its own challenges. A successful approach to this involves having the right team members, good leadership and a solid structure. An in-house team should be managed by someone with a good understanding of the ANCHOR elements. Depending on the size of the team, they may then manage other managers or team leaders who have specialist understanding of their own areas, and get involved in some of that work. For example, the SEO team and PPC team may each have their own manager or head of department, but it's important to make sure all of the different teams are working in conjunction with each other.

Even today, I see examples of SEO, PPC and other marketing teams being completely separate, each with no idea what the other team are doing. For example, an increase in branded PPC spend can have an impact on organic traffic; if the SEO team aren't aware of this activity, they can waste time trying to diagnose a drop in traffic that has a known internal cause. Data-sharing is often also lacking with teams that are isolated. If the PPC team are seeing great click-through rates for certain pages and ad copy, could those insights be shared to benefit organic optimisation?

Some businesses with in-house teams often choose to work with an agency too. This goes back to what I said earlier about not being able to do everything yourself and utilising the skillsets of others instead. If you have a great in-house team but lack high-level content or outreach skills, you may choose to hire an agency for support in those areas. You may have some requirements that don't constitute full-time roles and choose to hire agency or freelance staff to fulfil them. These staff should be treated as an arm of your current team and again it's good for that agency to be aware of other activity going on. Having this solid structure, with great leadership, can make for a successful team if they all work closely as a unit.

Pros

- Can manage the people and work easily, usually face to face

- Can hire in the required skills for the business

- The team have focus on that one business and should get to know the business well

Cons

- Costs of hiring and training

- Unexpected absences can put a hold on important work

- Hiring process can sometimes be long and frustrating, but is vital to get right

- Staff sometimes hired for functions that aren't necessarily full-time roles

Outsourcing

Outsourcing has become an increasingly popular term, especially with the rise of online platforms for this purpose. There are two main options for outsourcing: agencies and freelancers. Agencies vary from small specialist agencies such as content agencies, to huge full-service agencies that claim to do anything and everything marketing-related. The situation with freelancers is similar, on a much smaller scale. You might find freelancers specialising in a single area – such as content or Google Analytics – as well as more 'jack-of-all-trades' freelancers who manage the whole online marketing process. The latter category usually, and rightly, enlist the help of other freelancers to support the skills they lack. For example, when I was freelancing, I didn't write content. I'm not a wordsmith, but I know some excellent freelance writers; why would I spend hours writing content when I knew others who could do it better? Yes, I had to pay for that content, and sometimes it wasn't cheap. But it was about getting results rather than just pumping out cheap content so I could tick a task off a list. The good thing about managing that content myself, as opposed to having an in-house writer doing it with no input from me, was that I could ensure the topic was right, it wasn't conflicting with other content, it was optimised correctly, and so on.

Freelancers

Using freelancers can be a good option but I want to suggest avoiding the use of outsourcing platforms for online marketing services, especially SEO. Am I saying all SEO services on these platforms are terrible? No, of course not; there are some great freelancers on there, but finding them and trusting them is a whole other issue. There are huge numbers of marketers on those platforms claiming they can 'guarantee #1 rankings' and that they 'only use white hat methods'. I mentioned this earlier in the book, and I don't mean to sound like a broken record, but it's nonsense and gives our industry a bad name. They can't guarantee #1 results; no one can. And when you look into it, the examples they give of rankings they've achieved in the past are often for very specific things: 'guinea pig acupuncture in Buford' or 'tarot card reading in Wimbledon'. Local SEO is easier than ecommerce SEO and most of the examples you'll see are easy to achieve – and most likely irrelevant to your business's needs.

That said, I like some outsourcing platforms and I still use them for certain skillsets; one of my graphic designers is hired through one and she's great. The bottom line is that platforms can be fantastic but be careful what you use them for. It's hard to separate the wheat from the chaff, and there's a lot of chaff.

Now that my little rant about cheap freelancers is over, let's talk about the good ones. They're not going to wear the $5-per-hour price tag of some of the afore-mentioned services – but neither do they have to cost an arm and a leg.

It's important to look at their experience. How long have they been doing this? What have they done? What agencies, in-house teams and clients have they worked with? What results have they had? Recommendations also go a long way and can help you to put more trust in a freelancer.

You should remember that they need to be given time to get results – so make sure you're happy with your decisions and don't just think, 'I'll give them a try for a couple of months and see how it goes'. Also consider whether they're going to manage everything (even if they are using other freelancers), or if you're going to hire multiple freelancers, or whether you'll have one main freelancer managing several others. But if you hire multiple freelancers, make sure they're communicating and sharing in the same way that an in-house team would.

And that's how you should look at this: as an extension of your team. It can be a good option but bear in mind that you, or someone in your team, will have to manage them and ensure that your activity runs closely in line with theirs.

Pros

- Usually cheaper than agencies

- Can find specialist skills and experience

- No employee expenses like hiring, training, sickness and holiday pay

- Don't need to hire full-time

Cons

- Hard to find the right people

- If they go away or are sick, they may be unavailable – or may not come back at all

- They may not be completely on top of your industry or what's going on in your company (it's essential that you help them with this)

- If it's just one person managing everything, you're heavily reliant on them

- You still have one or more people to manage

Agencies

There are various sizes and business models that fall under the term 'agencies'. A one-man band could call himself an agency; another agency might employ thousands of staff. Some agencies have city offices all over the world and some adopt more of a remote working model. Some might only use full-time staff and some might use a mixture of employed staff and freelancers.

The other thing that varies greatly between agencies is the price tag. If an agency employs tens of thousands of people and is the most expensive option, does it make them the best? Absolutely not. Your budgets may well be a factor when choosing an agency but there are plenty of other considerations too:

- Do they have experience working with your type of business?

- What processes do they use?

- Does their offering sound realistic?

- What are the contract terms and how long are you tied in for?

It also helps to be aware of who will be involved in the campaign and what their level of experience is. Some agencies will take on a big client and then use junior staff to run most of it. When you're working with an agency, you want to be sure people with the right skill-sets and experience levels are involved in the relevant work for your business. If you want to know who's working on what within the agency you've hired, just ask. It's up to them to be transparent and reassure you that you're in safe and experienced hands.

Pros

- Team is usually managed for you by someone else

- No hiring issues – if someone leaves, the agency rehires

- Multiple skillsets

- No need to hire full-time staff for part-time roles; work is split internally among agency staff

- Not reliant on one person

Cons

- Usually more expensive than freelancers

- Can be hard to find the right agency for your business

You or a freelancer or an agency?

The obvious answer is: it depends. But I think I ruled out 'you' as a good option. Whatever your position in the business, you can't do all of this yourself. Whether that's down to skills or time, you can't be an engineer, mechanic, artist and statistician and you can't work eight days a week!

That leaves us with freelancers and agencies as outsourcing options. The main considerations are then: budgets, requirements, time and resources. You may have the budget for an agency, but is it right for you? What are your requirements? Can you find someone to get you the desired results? Do you have the time to manage multiple freelancers or would an agency be a better option? Do you have someone in-house that could be the central point of contact for the agency or would it have to be you? It also depends on your current resources. If you have a full in-house team but need content support, would a freelancer suffice, or would an agency be a better option? That may depend on the quantity required, too. One freelancer can only do so much. Some questions that may help you decide:

- Do we need support with everything or just with one or two skillsets?

- Can our requirements be done by one person or do we need a team?

- Do we have the time to manage multiple out-sourced staff?

- What are our priorities and who is best placed to help with them?

It also goes without saying that it's important to make sure whoever you work with is a good fit. Whether it's a potential in-house employee, a freelancer or an agency, be sure to meet them – or at least have a video call – and make sure they're personable and a good fit for your business's culture. If you've chosen well,

you're going to be working with them for a long time
so you need to maximise the chances of a good working
relationship.

Conclusion

Whether you plan to implement a lot of this yourself or have your team do it for you, understanding the contents of this book will arm you with the knowledge you need to take the next steps. SEO and the complementary channels we discussed can be a real force to be reckoned with when they're used correctly. Using the ANCHOR method will help you to simplify your strategy and ensure you're doing all that you should be to grow online.

It's not too late

I often speak to business owners who are unsure what to do next. Some have seen traffic flatlining for two years; some have seen constant declines. Some have even seen gradual growth and then a big dip. I spoke to someone who said she was 'firefighting with Google algorithm updates'. I speak to a lot of people who have seen huge declines off the back of a migration. It's painful to see such declines – but it's not too late to sort it.

If you're flatlining, declining, or even just not seeing the levels of growth you want, chances are that something is wrong. Something is missing. You need to troubleshoot problems, ensure you're using the right strategies and tactics, and make sure there are enough of them. You won't see an overnight recovery or overnight success – but do things right, and you will soon see the impact of your hard work.

The ecommerce scorecard

This set of questions is designed to score your current online strategies and benchmark you against where you should be. Are you doing all you can for your ecommerce business, or are you leaving money on the table?

http://bit.ly/ecommerce-scorecard

Glossary

3xx redirect These response codes are usually used when changing a URL for some reason (eg a migration). They direct search engines and users to the new page. The most common are 301 (permanent redirects) and 302 (temporary redirects).

404 error The response code for 'Page Not Found'. This will be served if a page is broken or doesn't exist.

Above/below the fold The fold is the lowest area of the screen that is visible without scrolling. Everything above this is above the fold. If you need to scroll down, you're then looking below the fold.

Alt tag An HTML attribute that is added to images on a webpage. This is the text that is displayed when an image can't be shown and is also useful to advise search engines as to what the image shows.

Anchor text The clickable text that is used in a link.

Article spinning An old SEO tactic that involved rewritten words and/or sentences, resulting in multiple versions of the same article. These 'unique' versions would then usually be syndicated out to various places across the web.

Black hat Black hat SEO is a term referring to SEO tactics which are against Google guidelines. Many people would argue that black hat is more related to illegal tactics (such as hacking sites) and pushing the boundaries of Google guidelines is grey hat. Sticking very closely to Google guidelines is considered white hat.

Bounce rate The percentage of users who leave the website after visiting just one page.

Breadcrumbs A breadcrumb or breadcrumb trail is a type of navigation often used between a website's main navigation and the main content of the page.

Cannibalisation Cannibalisation or conflict is when two or more pages are competing for the same search terms.

Canonical tag An HTML element that tells search engines the preferred/master version of a page. Often used to avoid duplication.

Crawl error An error that occurs when a search engine bot tries to crawl a page/pages on a website (eg 404 error).

Disavow file A file that is uploaded to Google to request it to ignore the contained list of backlinks.

Hreflang Hreflang tags are used by websites serving multiple languages and/or countries, to tell search engines which pages to serve to which languages/regions.

IFTTT syndication If This Then That (IFTTT) is an online tool used to trigger actions in integrated apps based on certain conditions. IFTTT syndication is used to automatically publish content to a variety of platforms.

Index bloat An issue when a website has too many pages indexed by search engines (pages that shouldn't be indexed).

Link spam Links created to manipulate search engine ranking algorithms.

Nofollow The nofollow tag tells search engines, such as Google, not to follow the link and pass link value.

Noindex The noindex tag is used to tell search engines not to include that page in their index/search results.

Organic traffic Traffic from search engines.

Overall traffic All traffic, from all acquisition channels (eg organic, paid, email, social and so on.)

SSL SSL is a technology used to secure connections between websites and users. A website uses an SSL certificate to ensure the safety of a user's data such as payment details or personal data.

Title tag An HTML element used to tell users (and search engines) what a page is about. The title tag of a page is usually what is displayed as the main title in search engine results.

References

Printed sources

Clear, J., *Atomic Habits: An Easy and Proven Way to Build Good Habits and Break Bad Ones* (Random House Business, 2018).

Online sources

AdStage, *Q4 2018 Benchmark Report* (2018) https://cdn2.hubspot.net/hubfs/4350015/Q4%202018%20Paid%20Media%20Benchmark%20Report%20(2).pdf

Adthena, 'The Rise of Google Shopping', *Adthena Search Advertising Report* (2018) https://cdn2.hubspot

.net/hubfs/546369/Gated%20Content%20PDFs/Adthena
-Google-Shopping-Report-2018.pdf

BrightEdge, 'Organic Search Is Still the Largest Channel' (2017 report) https://brightedge.com/resources
/research-reports/content-optimization

Campaign Monitor, 'Year in Review', *Annual Report*
(2016) https://campaignmonitor.com/company/annual
-report/2016

Cutts, M., 'Gadgets, Google, and SEO: The decay and
fall of guest blogging for SEO' (Google/SEO, 2014)
https://mattcutts.com/blog/guest-blogging

Cutts, M., 'Is there a version of Google that excludes
backlinks as a ranking factor?' (YouTube, 2014) www
.youtube.com/watch?v=NCY3oWhI2og

Dean, B., 'Linking Building Case Study: How I Increased
My Search Traffic by 110% in 14 Days' (Backlinko, 2016)
https://backlinko.com/skyscraper-technique

DMA National Client Email Report (emailmonday, 2015)
https://emailmonday.com/dma-national-client-email
-report-2015

Dobson, C., 'Study: 71% of Amazon Advertisers Spend 25% of Digital Ad Budgets on Amazon' (LSA Insider, 2018) https://lsainsider.com/study-71-of-amazon -advertisers-spend-25-of-digital-ad-budgets-on-amazon /archives

Dolliver, M., 'Some Bad (and Good) News for Facebook in 2019' (Marketer, 2019) https://emarketer.com /content/predicting-some-bad-news-and-good-news -for-facebook-in-2019

Gabbert, E., '5 Reasons to Diversify Your Search Strategy with PPC Advertising' (WordStream, 2015) https:// wordstream.com/blog/ws/2012/07/18/diversify-search -strategy-ppc

Gesenhues, A., 'Amazon reports 3rd straight quarter of triple-digit ad revenue growth' (Martech: Management, 2018) https://martechtoday.com/amazon-reports -3rd-straight-quarter-of-triple-digit-ad-revenue-growth -227047

Internet Live Stats https://internetlivestats.com/one -second/#google-band

Irvine, M., 'Google Ads Benchmarks for YOUR Industry [Updated!]: Paid Search Marketing', *The WordStream*

Blog (WordStream, 2019) https://wordstream.com/blog /ws/2016/02/29/google-adwords-industry-benchmarks

Irvine, M., 'Google Ads Benchmarks for YOUR Industry [Updated!]: Social Media', *The WordStream Blog* (WordStream, 2019) https://wordstream.com/blog/ws /2017/02/28/facebook-advertising-benchmarks

Prater, J. D., *Q4 2017 Paid Search and Paid Social Benchmark Report* (AdStage, 2017) https://cdn2.hubspot.net /hubfs/4350015/Benchmark%20Report/AdStage%20Q4 %20%20PPC%20Benchmark%20Report.pdf

Slater, M., 'Olympic cycling: Marginal gains underpin Team GB dominance' (BBC Sport, 2012) www.bbc.co .uk/sport/olympics/19174302

Slegg, J., *Facebook Retail Advertisers Averaging 152% ROI Report* (Search Engine Watch, 2013) https:// searchenginewatch.com/sew/study/2301423/facebook -retail-advertisers-averaging-152-roi-report

Soames, C., 'Google Ads conversion rate averages by industry' (SmartInsights, 2018) https://smartinsights .com/paid-search-marketing-ppc/paid-search-display -network/google-adwords-conversion-rate-averages-by -industry-infographic

Sullivan, D., 'Meet RankBrain: The Artificial Intelligence That's Now Processing Google Search Results' (SearchEngineLand, 2015) https://searchengineland.com/meet-rankbrain-google-search-results-234386

The Badger, 'Amazon Advertising Stats: 2019 Update' (AdBadger, 2019) https://adbadger.com/blog/amazon-advertising-stats

Acknowledgements

This book wouldn't have been possible without these amazing people.

First and foremost, thank you to my wife, Carla. I wouldn't be able to do any of this without you. You're an incredible person and your support means the world to me. Also, thanks to my wonderful children. You're my motivation and I love you to the moon and back!

Thanks to my phenomenal brothers and sister, as well as my wider family and friends. You've been a huge part of who I am as a person today. So it's your fault.

Thanks to the Wild Sprout team. You guys are awesome and I see exciting times ahead.

Thank you to Kirsty Hulse, Kelvin Newman and Daniel Priestley for your invaluable support and advice. And thanks to my accountability group. You continue to drive me in the right direction and I'm lucky to have such great minds to tap into.

Thank you to my publishers, Lucy, Joe and Helen. Thanks for the advice and constant feedback. You're a pleasure to work with.

Thank you to everyone I've worked with. I've learned so much from all of you and the contents of this book are from a combination of experiences with you guys.

And last but not least, thanks to anyone reading this book. It means so much that you've taken the time to read it and I wish you every success with your business. Now get out there and become a force to be reckoned with!

The Author

M artin Hayman has worked in digital marketing for over ten years and his experience has seen him become known in some circles for technical SEO, auditing and migrations. He has worked on a huge number of successful campaigns and projects, across both client side and agency side roles.

After starting his agency Wild Sprout, Martin created the ANCHOR model and has used it to help ecommerce businesses and other large websites turn things around and grow their online presence. He has also spoken at industry events and provided training to various businesses and agencies.

Outside of SEO and the digital marketing world, Martin is a family-first guy. He used to fight in cages, but now he just sticks to Jiu Jitsu.

Connect with Martin Hayman

in Martin Hayman
◎ martinhayman
𝕏 @martinhayman
⊕ www.martinhayman.com

Connect with Wild Sprout

in Wild Sprout
◎ wearewildsprout
𝕏 @wearewildsprout
f wearewildsprout
⊕ wildsprout.digital

Lightning Source UK Ltd.
Milton Keynes UK
UKHW020005080919
349327UK00013B/1170/P